FLYER

Part One: The War Years

By

D. Pembroke Neff

For Devon, Catesby, Alex and Chase

Table of Contents

Chapter One

As the last period bell rang, I ran into the classroom and sat in my usual seat in the back row, next to Freddy. Mr. West, our comparative religion teacher, was writing on the blackboard. Betty Simpson, the doll-faced girl of many of my most recent erotic dreams, turned in her seat and smiled at me.

My stomach flip-flopped. I felt dirty and confused. Here I was sitting in class about to hear another inspiring and impassioned lecture on the suffering of the Buddha, and all I could think about was feeling Betty's magnificent milky white tits.

Were all seventeen-year-olds so horny? Envisioning Betty naked made sitting uncomfortable. I prayed no one asked me to stand up for anything. That wouldn't be good. Something else not so good—only one week until graduation and I was still a virgin. Up until now Betty had only allowed me to second base, but somehow, deep down inside, we both knew she was going to be the one.

Freddy interrupted my lascivious thoughts by handing me a note.

You touch her tits yet?

My cheeks blushed as I looked around at my fellow classmates, hoping that none of them had seen what Freddy had written. I balled up the note and shook my head then stared straight ahead.

Betty, the girl I lusted after, and Dot, the girl whose cherry Freddy had picked about a month ago, had been the subjects of most of our discussions over the last month. I'd told him that Betty and I were getting really close to doing it and that I planned to make it happen soon. Freddy, now safely at home base, was eager to help me score as well.

Freddy elbowed me, looked at the wadded up note then raised an eyebrow. Apparently he expected an answer. Or maybe he was puzzled about why I'd crumpled the note.

I waved him off and tried to focus on Mr. West and what he was saying about next week's graduation ceremony.

"I expect to see everyone at the Baccalaureate Sermon next Thursday evening. Be in your assigned seats in the auditorium, no later than 5:45. The service starts promptly at 6." Mr. West underlined the date and time on the board. "Oh, and remember, due to OPA regulations concerning the use of gas, cars may not be driven either to the Baccalaureate Sermon or the commencement exercises the next night. If you ride a school bus, your bus will make its regular run that afternoon to transport seniors, their families, members of the glee club and band to the school for the evening's activities."

Yeah, it wasn't like I had a father who could attend. Or a car to drive, and it was quite possible that my mother wouldn't be able to come either. Dad had disappeared when I was thirteen, so Mom was always picking up odd jobs here and there in an attempt to save for my college tuition. She worked hard, very hard, sometimes even at night.

Freddy and I and all of our friends walked everywhere worth walking to, which actually didn't amount to much in a small southern California town. We had a few stores and churches and two schools—the grammar school and high school—and we had the Palace Theater, which supplied us with the only real fun in town. If I'd had more money, I'd have watched every movie that ever played there. As it was, I was lucky to see a couple of movies every few months.

Besides, I didn't have much free time. Seemed like I was always working on my artwork or spending time in church to please my mom. I spent a lot of time in church.

Freddy slid another note my way.

Which movie should we take the girls to see tonight? *One of Our Aircraft is Missing* or *Song of the Islands?*

I wanted to see the action movie about downed flyers trying to survive in enemy territory and I was willing to bet that Freddy did too. But Dot wanted to see the musical. Oh well, Betty Grable was in it so I could put up with the singing and dancing just to get a look at her spectacular gams. The newspaper recently reported that her legs had been insured by Lloyd's of London for $1 million. They were said to be the ideal proportion: thigh—18.5 inches; calf—12 inches; and ankle—7.5 inches. Whatever, it all sounded perfect to me. And maybe afterward, Betty would be in the mood for—

Freddy's elbow jolted me back into reality. "Well?" he mouthed.

I circled *Song of the Islands* and turned the note so he could see it.

His disappointment was obvious. Both of us enjoyed war movies and *One of Our Aircraft is Missing* promised to be filled with nonstop action, but I was trying to get laid. I needed a movie about romance, not war. Maybe we could see the other movie later, when we'd saved up enough money. I'd always thought that it would be pretty neat to be an aviator. I bet those flyboys never had trouble getting laid.

Only one week until graduation and my eighteenth birthday. Maybe then, Betty would finally wave me around third base and into home plate. I stared at her while she sat at her desk and tried to imagine what real live sex felt like. It had to feel great.

Oh man, who was I kidding? Betty wasn't the one holding things back. I'd been the one reluctant to put the moves on her. In fact, she probably wondered why I hadn't pursued her harder. If I held back much longer she might start to think that I was a queer.

Truth was, I wasn't a fruit. I just didn't want to get myself tied down, and knocking up a girl was the surest way to make that happen. If the rubber broke and the rabbit died, I'd be screwed forever, destined to live out the rest of my life in this festering shithole of a town. Nope, I had plans, big plans and, as much as I craved Betty, those plans didn't include her.

Of course I could probably survive, at least a little while without having sex, but I would absolutely snap my cap if I wasn't able to get out of this jerkwater town soon. I desperately wanted a scholarship to art school and I wanted to experience all the things that this tiny town never had to offer.

I was probably fooling myself about going to art school. Although my mother had worked long hours to help pay for my tuition, the reality was that college was expensive and unless I got some serious financial help, my matriculation didn't look promising. My mother saw college as a safe haven that might keep me out of the war. I saw it as my ticket out of here.

I glanced at Freddy.

He was drawing pictures of airplanes on his homework assignment. Being the world renowned pervert that he was, Freddy had turned the engines underneath the wings into gigantic tits with propellers attached to the nipples. He had scribbled 'The Ultra-Bosomed Flying Fortress' in large black letters at the bottom of the page.

Freddy was probably my best friend. I'd known him since we were kids. But come on now, didn't he realize how totally lame that plane looked?

I quickly moved my pencil across my own paper. In no time I'd sketched the exact replica of a Messerschmitt BF-109 that I'd seen in the movie *Captain of the Clouds* a year earlier.

Freddy reached over and snatched the picture off of my desk. And sure enough about a minute later, the Messerschmitt BF-109 instead of having its engine in the nose-cone at the front, was now sporting gigantic tit engines under its wings.

I rolled my eyes. Could it be that I was outgrowing Freddy? I sighed and forced myself to listen to Mr. West as he droned on about the Buddha.

"The son of a king, the Buddha abandoned a life of pleasure to find enlightenment. But he soon learned that life is qualified by suffering," Mr. West underlined the last word. "Suffering has a cause. Suffering ends when one learns how to give up whatever it is to which they are too attached. Giving up attachments can only come from sacrifice." His chalk squeaked when he put three lines under the word sacrifice.

"This is not unlike Christian teachings as they relate to Jesus on the cross. His personal suffering ended when he was able to give up his attachment to his mortal life and accept the fate that had been decreed by the Father. This sacrifice was made in order to end the eternal suffering of all those believers bathed in the holy water of baptism."

Towards the end of Mr. West's lecture, I looked around the room, at the rest of my classmates. Many of them were struggling to pay attention, their eyes were glassed over and their bodies swayed back and forth in their seats as if they were just about to fall out of consciousness. I thought to myself, a lot of my own suffering came as a result of being stuck in this God forsaken town with these God forsaken imbeciles. I would have no trouble breaking my attachment to this place. In fact, I couldn't wait to do it, and about the biggest sacrifice I'd have to make would be that I'd never get the opportunity to give Betty Simpson the fuck of a lifetime.

Chapter Two

After the graduation ceremony, Freddy and I and our friend Ralph Jefferson changed out of our nice clothes and into casual pants and Hawaiian shirts. Ralph had a car. Lucky bastard. He was one of the few kids at school who had access to a car and enough gas ration stamps to keep it moving.

In celebration of my eighteenth birthday, the three of us drove to our favorite nightclub–Pete's Bar and Grill. It featured a large outdoor stone patio that overlooked the Pacific Ocean. Two painted cow skulls with flowers for eyes hung on the wall next to an old picture of a guy surfing. I think his name was Tom Blake. He was a good looking guy and stylish too. With his hair swept back and his incredible physique, he looked like Tarzan riding the wave.

We arrived just as the sun was setting. I could smell the salt air as the steady breeze ballooned out my baggy shirt. Large waves were crashing on the shore nearby.

"What a great place," I said.

Freddy pointed at the ceiling, where strings of colored Christmas lights strung along the rafters danced in the wind. "Check it out."

Sandy, the bar owner, sidled alongside of us. "You like it? I put 'em up in honor of your birthday."

"It's swell, Sandy. Thanks." I shook his outstretched hand. "But you didn't need to go to such bother."

He clapped me on the back. "No bother at all, son. Your pops would have wanted you to have something special for your eighteenth birthday."

"Yeah." I looked down at my feet. Sandy and my dad had been best friends since forever, until Dad had walked out on all of us.

Sandy cleared his throat. "Four ice cold Schlitz beers here," he hollered to one of the waitresses. After we finished the first round, the bar started to fill up and Sandy pushed away from the table and stood up. "Beers on the house tonight, boys."

Bing Crosby's *I'll Be Seeing You* played on the jukebox as he slipped away to tend bar.

My friends and I drank seven beers apiece. I threw up four times that night. It was a great night! At least the part I remember was.

The United States government sent me a belated birthday gift three days later. When the letter fell through the mail slot in our front door, all of my plans for art school and chasing women vanished.

Alex Anderson, report for training and service in the U.S. Army on 20 July 1944.

What the hell . . . ? I'd been drafted.

Not exactly the way I had envisioned getting out of this boring town but a way out, nevertheless. The downside, of course, was that we were at war and the chances of me getting injured or killed had just gone up dramatically.

Shit, how could I be drafted? I was still a virgin.

I'd seen the newsreels of the fighting oversees, and I wanted no part of any of it. My mouth was suddenly so dry that my tongue felt like it was glued to my palate. Heart racing, my vision started to blur and I became lightheaded.

I wasn't ready to die.

For many people who believe in resurrection, death is inconsequential. It isn't seen as an ending, but rather as a new beginning. A second life of blissful happiness for all eternity. Like most of my friends, I went to church every

Sunday because it was just something that folks did. But as far as believing in the whole life after death thing, well, that part had always been a little questionable for me.

I wanted to believe, but hell, I wasn't even sure about things going on in my own little world let alone about things in the infinite cosmic world of the heavens. Of course, like most people, I lived my life as if God existed, but in many ways it was simply Pascal's Wager. I had convinced myself it was better to believe in something and find out there's nothing rather than believe in nothing and find out there's something.

Joining the army was something I had little knowledge about and even less desire to engage in. Dying in war, no matter how noble the cause, was definitely not on my list of things to do, even if I might be resurrected when all was said and done.

Though I couldn't do anything about being drafted, I figured I should do whatever I could to improve my chances for survival. So, the day before I shipped out, I went to a tattoo parlor near Los Angeles and instructed the owner to put a small black cross just above my right wrist. I'm not sure why I chose the symbol of Christ, but it just felt like the right thing to do. And in the end, even though the artist had tried to talk me into getting 'MOM' inked across my upper arm, I insisted on the cross. That way every time I looked at it, I'd be reminded that in the midst of physical life, we were always surrounded by spiritual death and that the solution to all of the madness in our lives might just be through the cross.

Little did I know then, but my life would soon be altered by that simple little black-inked symbol just above my wrist.

Chapter Three

At the end of fifteen weeks of basic training, Army Air Corps Captain Jim Franklin stopped me on the way to the mess hall. "You interested in flying, Anderson?"

Was hell hot? Of course I was interested. Everyone knew it was a lot safer up in a plane than down on the ground with the rest of the grunts fighting for their lives on some distant battlefield.

"Yes, sir," I said, snapping to attention and trying not to grin.

Aptitude tests I'd taken at the beginning of basic training had revealed my abilities to draw and to recreate precise sketches of things I'd seen only briefly.

So, before I could even muster up a good fart, I was a Private First Class in the 408th Bomb Squadron, 22nd Bomb Group that was deploying to Brisbane, Australia. Our squadron's commanding officer, Lt. Colonel Brian O. Miller had requested that I be given specialized training on a recently developed bombsight called the Blue Ox.

If I successfully completed this training I would be promoted to a Technical Sergeant and that meant more money in my pocket. Who could argue with that?

The Blue Ox, as I later learned, had been around since 1941. The Air Corps had first deployed it on its B-17 bombers. It allowed our boys to strike enemy targets with exceptional precision from extremely high altitudes. Known by its secret code name the Blue Ox, the device was otherwise known as the Norden Bombsight.

Bombers using this new and improved bombsight could accurately hit targets to within seventy five feet from an altitude of thirty thousand feet, and most incredibly, this was accomplished by linking the Norden Bombsight to the plane's autopilot.

During training we were sworn to secrecy about the details of the Blue Ox and the Air Corps made sure that we would never allow it to fall into enemy hands should the bomber crash or get shot down. We even had to sign an oath to that effect.

Technical Sergeants, such as I hoped to become, had sole responsibility for the destruction of the Blue Ox in the event of a crash. We were to shoot the Norden Bombsight in order to dismantle it and then we were supposed to set off an internal thermite grenade that would melt it completely from the inside out.

It sounded good in theory, but in all practicality, this scared the crap out of me. I was just an aspiring teenage artist. My main objective in life prior to all of this top-secret bullshit, was trying to get laid—a feat that although I had come extremely close to accomplishing with Betty Simpson, still sadly eluded me.

Despite my misgivings, I successfully completed the training program in December of 1944. After a few of weeks of badly needed R&R, the 408th shipped out to Brisbane, Australia in late January of 1945. The 408th Squadron, to which I was attached, was soon temporarily relocated to the north, to an airfield along the Reid River, near Townsville. Eventually, the squadron was moved permanently to an area just north of Darwin, in order to be closer to Japanese military targets in Borneo and New Guinea.

Chapter Four

Our plane was called *Betty Grable's Ass*. Go figure!

Someone had painted her iconic bathing suit picture onto its left side, just underneath the pilot's window.

In the photograph, Betty was posed in a bathing suit, body turned away from the camera, gorgeous face peering over her right shoulder. In the recreation adorning our plane, the artist had somehow forgotten to paint on her swimsuit! I mean she was as naked as the day she was born. Her big beautiful round ass was poking out all over the place. We were the most talked about plane in the squadron.

I can't tell you the number of times men passed by our plane and yelled out things like, "Man, I'd bite into that ass like it was a steak sandwich."

Given the chance, I would have, too!

Our squadron's commanding officer, Lt. Colonel Miller, ordered us to paint over it numerous times whenever visiting dignitaries glimpsed it, but he always winked when they weren't looking, letting us know that it was A-Okay for the painting to remain just the way it was.

The mission of the 408th Bomb Squadron was to attack Japanese targets, primarily oil refinery installations, on the island of Borneo and provide aerial support for any Australian or Allied forces in the area. Our usual flight path took us west northwest over the tip of northern Australia, toward the island of Sulawesi. Continuing northwest we flew over Palu, toward Borneo and the South China Sea. Once we reached the coast we turned southwest toward Bangka and then eventually southeastward back toward home. In essence we flew in a giant elongated loop.

Of the many missions we'd already completed in the region, we'd only used the Norden Bombsight twice—

once in western Borneo when we attacked the Ishiban oil refinery near Pontianak and then once again when we attacked a Japanese sub base near the Banda Sea.

Our mission on 31 May, 1945 started out just like all the others before it. I'd been in Australia for almost four months. On that day, we were to complete our infamous elongated loop to the South China Sea, drop ordinance on a small Japanese supply base north of Kuching, and return home. The weather promised perfect flying conditions, and the absence of heavy, low-lying cloud formations would make our target much easier to see.

Despite the fact that it was eighty-five degrees Fahrenheit outside, each of the crew wore Blue Bunny flight suits—a glorified electric blanket vaguely shaped like a one-piece flight suit to keep us warm at high altitude. Over top of the flight suit, I had pants and leather flight jacket. I wore heavy insulated boots and used leather gloves insulated with wool to keep my hands comfortable. I topped off the uniform with my parachute harness and a B3 inflatable life preserver that everyone called a "Mae West" in honor of her famously buxom figure.

By the time I was dressed I was sweating like a pig and stewing in my own juices. Still, it couldn't be helped. The excessive layers of clothing would keep me from freezing my ass off later and all the gear just might save my life if it should come to that.

At an altitude of thirty thousand feet, it wasn't unusual for the temperature inside the plane to fall to ten below zero since the bomber was unpressurized and had little to no insulation. I lumbered toward the plane, carrying my rubber oxygen mask, goggles, leather helmet, and a forty two pound flak jacket.

Of course, the Blue Bunny was also like a sponge, even now absorbing the sweat that would eventually begin to freeze once we broke through ten thousand feet. It was always a gamble as to whether or not any of us would get shocked or burn ourselves when we plugged in the Blue Bunny suits. Water and electricity aren't the best of friends, and when they combine over top of your private parts, well, let's just say, it isn't a pleasant experience. Each of the crew had suffered some type of skin burn or mild shock at one time or the other. 'Freezing and frying, freezing and frying,' was the mantra we often chanted in unison.

We didn't like it, but we couldn't do anything about it. We had to do what we could to stay warm.

When we neared ten thousand feet, our pilot, Captain William "Wild Bill" McKinerney, radioed to all of us that it was time to put on our oxygen masks and hook into the plane's oxygen system. Since the plane was not pressurized, at heights of ten thousand feet or more, everyone would pass out without the oxygen in less than a minute and a half. Three minutes without oxygen and we'd all die.

I pressed my mask firmly against my face and deeply inhaled the rubbery smelling air.

As we continued our ascent, Captain Frank Webster, our co-pilot, radio checked-in on each of us every fifteen minutes to make sure we were all still conscious. We had to respond when our name was called.

"Tech Sergeant Anderson report," he'd ask.

"Tech Sergeant Anderson reporting," I'd reply

The monotony and routine of it all got old, but at the same time it was reassuring and comforting to know that everyone was okay.

During our climb, Captain Webster would tell us when to plug in our Blue Bunny suits. As I pushed the plug into the plane's electrical socket, I held my breath, waiting for sparks to fly and receive the shock of a lifetime.

Nothing. Thank God. I looked around to see if everyone else had been so lucky. It appeared that everyone was okay, so far, so good.

We reached our destination a couple of hours later. Everything went according to plans. After dropping our bombs precisely on the mark, we made our long turn back home, banking out briefly over the South China Sea.

Within a few minutes, *Betty Grable's Ass* began a rapid descent from her usual bombing altitude. I felt my ears pop as I unplugged my Blue Bunny suit. I swallowed hard to try to unblock my ears. It took a few moments, but soon I could hear clearly again.

"Work's done, boys. It's time for a little fun," Captain Wild Bill screamed to us.

Betty Grable's Ass continued to drop lower and lower, moving closer and closer to the ocean.

"Masks off, boys," Wild Bill said at last. "The peep show of Borneo will commence in three, two, one. . ." Wild Bill then banked the plane hard to the left as he flew even lower, over top a familiar native village on the white sand beach, near Bintulu.

The entire crew moved quickly to the left side of the plane. It was a wonder we didn't roll completely over.

A few hundred feet below us, the so-called Sea Dayak women of Malaysian Borneo went about their daily chores, completely topless. The only ones who covered their breasts either had huge bosoms or were old ladies with what we called 'saggy bags.'

Perky, brown bosoms jiggled everywhere below us. We flew so low it felt like I could reach out and squeeze them. The guys around me whistled and hooted and yelled out crude comments.

The peep show of Borneo was one of those simple little things that we all looked forward to. We'd seen it several times but never tired of it. Like the caged animals we were, we each allowed our hormones to rage shamelessly. Hell, this was the closest thing we had to sex.

"All right," I yelled. "Long live the peep show of Borneo."

Usually when we flew over the girls they looked up and waved and sometimes even blew us kisses. Today, however, only a few of them bothered to look up and those who did simply stared at us as if they were in a trance. One girl mysteriously had her arms raised and seemed to be frantically motioning at us to go away. I couldn't figure out what she meant. At that instant all hell broke loose.

"Holy shit, JAPS!" Captain Wild Bill yelled into the plane's radio intercom.

Right where the beach ended and the green jungle overtook the sand, all the way down to the water's edge, were a dozen Jap soldiers with their weapons raised skyward. They began a rapid fire assault on our plane. Small arms fragments raked the aircraft.

Wild Bill pulled back the plane's steering yoke with all his might, and we slowly started to bank up and out over the azure colored ocean.

Then we heard a chilling sound, one that each of us knew all too well—the clack, clack, clack, of a .50 caliber Jap machine gun. By this time I'd already jumped back to my side of the plane and was frantically searching for my flak jacket. I'd tossed it on the floor with my mask, goggles, and gloves. Shrapnel was exploding throughout the cockpit. Sparks were flying everywhere and within seconds *Betty Grable's Ass* began to fill with smoke. This can't be happening I thought. It seemed unreal.

We were unable to return fire because all of our gunners had left their turrets in order to see the semi-naked girls. Not that it really mattered at this point. We'd already been hit hard by the Japs, and taking out those little Nips now, even if we could, seemed pointless. We were now fighting to stay aloft. It was a losing effort.

The plane started to roll slowly to the right.

"What's happening?" I yelled out to Wild Bill.

I looked up toward the cockpit when he didn't answer.

He'd been shot through the left side of his neck and was bleeding profusely. The white silk scarf he was wearing began turning crimson as his blood seeped into it.

Wild Bill took a shuddering breath and then his chest dropped for the final time.

Shit, our pilot was dead and *Betty Grable's Ass*, was headed straight into the sea.

Captain Webster struggled to keep the plane aloft while I tried to regain my composure. Being in an airplane spinning out of control with men screaming for their lives, with foul smelling electrical smoke filling the cabin, and with a dead pilot at the helm was the most helpless feeling I could ever imagine.

Since the floatation devices had been removed from the wings of *Betty Grable's Ass* per protocol for all planes equipped with the Norden Bombsight, the plane and all its secrets would soon be on the bottom of the ocean. Nevertheless, as instructed, I took out my pistol and shot at the Norden Bombsight and then set off its internal thermite grenade, completely melting its inside components.

At that point the plane started to roll upside down.

I threw myself into my seat and buckled in. When the plane was completely upside down, the vast blueness of the ocean seemed to be coming directly at us at an accelerated pace.

When the plane smashed into the water, everything suddenly went black.

The fuselage was ripped completely in half, and the top of the plane had been peeled back like a sardine can. Because the section I was in had righted itself in the water shortly after we hit, the sun was now shining directly in my face. I was still buckled in my seat when I came to. For a moment, it was eerily quiet except for the hissing and gulping sound of the plane taking on water.

"Help!"

I swiveled my head and tried to locate the sound.

"Over here!"

The garbled voice belonged to our tail gunner, Eddie Smith. He was tangled in a mess of wires and couldn't free himself. He was located in the other half of the wreckage, maybe fifty feet away.

I unbuckled my belt and began moving toward him, crawling over the wreckage within the plane. Before I knew it, the rate at which *Betty Grable's Ass* was filling with water had greatly accelerated. I no longer had to struggle through wrecked plane parts. Now I could swim over them. Unfortunately, this meant that Eddie was getting farther away from me with each passing second as his part of the plane continued to rapidly sink. It wasn't long before all I could see of Eddie was the top of his hair. I was never going to get to him before the plane completely disappeared under the water, taking Eddie with it.

By the time I reached the place where I'd last seen him, Eddie was completely gone. I put my face under the water and searched for him. Eddie and the rest of my buddies continued their swift decent into the dark blue abyss. Eyes opened wide and still horribly entangled in the wires, Eddie stared directly up at me. His mouth was wildly contorted and he seemed to be screaming at the top of his lungs and yet I heard nothing. The only thing I saw were air bubbles escaping from his mouth.

As if in a dream, a large Manta ray appeared by his side. Eddie's head suddenly turned in its direction then whipped back toward me as if to ask if this was really happening. The ray slowly glided through the water just like we had glided through the air only minutes earlier.

My lungs began to burn.

I lifted my head out of the water and took in a huge breath of fresh air. When I put my face back in again, Eddie and the rest of my crewmates were gone.

The military had been very efficient in its effort to prevent our equipment from falling into the hands of the Japanese. By removing all flotation devices from the wings of the B-26, it had sunk like a stone.

No doubt, the Japs had seen our plane go down, but they probably didn't know exactly where it had crashed and, with any luck, would never find it at the bottom of the ocean. We'd probably flown at least fifteen miles away from them while struggling to keep the plane aloft.

Because of the rugged terrain and lack of roads the Japs would have a hard time getting to the crash site quickly. However, since Japanese patrol boats were often seen in this vicinity, I needed to get onto dry land ASAP.

Could I swim to safety wearing a flight suit, helmet, boots, jacket and pants? Not likely. My soaked clothing alone added at least forty pounds to my weight. Thank God I hadn't put the flak jacket on or else I'd be at the bottom of the ocean with the rest of my crew. I stripped off as much of the dead weight as I could.

I then pulled the two cords on the upper edge of my life preserver, each of which were connected to small cartridges of fluid carbon dioxide. This triggered the fluid carbon dioxide to turn into a gas that then filled up the vest's air pockets.

"You've got to be fucking kidding," I muttered.

My life vest had been badly punctured during the crash. The carbon dioxide was now pouring out with a dreadful hiss. My vest was now useless.

As I treaded water, I tried to measure the distance to the nearest land. The mountains and beach appeared to be a few miles away. Hell, they could have been ten miles away for all I really knew. Measuring distance, while bobbing in the ocean, was a nearly impossible feat. And even if I did reach the land, the area was soon to be swarming with enemy soldiers searching for me. My options weren't good. I had to try to swim for land.

Off to my right, not far away, I spotted what looked like a fin cutting through the water. It disappeared quickly. My vision blurred. Blood ran down my forehead into my eyes.

Things were quickly going from bad to worse. My head was cut pretty badly, I probably had a concussion, and now I was equipped with absolutely nothing to keep me afloat.

In a race between danger and indecision, the difference between life and death came down to confidence, faith in one's own abilities and certainty in one's self. I wasn't certain that I could make the swim, but I knew with absolute knowledge that if I didn't try, I'd soon drown or be eaten by sharks. I'd just have to trust that I could evade the enemy once I got to land.

I began to swim as best as I could. Grab pull, grab pull, grab pull, on and on it went. Every so often I stopped and treaded water as I looked toward the beach to see how much farther I had to go.

About halfway there I couldn't go any farther. My head throbbed, blood was everywhere, and I was now extremely nauseated. I looked from side to side, not sure if I was searching for an angel to rescue me or a shark to eat me. Either way, I'd find relief from the suffering.

My eyes closed. Now, more than ever, I needed surcease from pain. I just needed a small rest, a tiny little rest and then I would continue on.

My eyes opened and my arms began moving in synchronized strokes once again. "I will endure, I will survive, and I will not be broken!" I chanted to myself.

Off in the distance, over to my left, I noticed the ocean's swells almost breaking in a specific area. The waves would feather along the top, but not completely break. The water there seemed slightly turbulent and was a lighter color than the rest of the ocean.

Could a reef be there, slightly submerged? If I could get there, and if it was indeed a reef, it might be shallow enough for me to stand on and rest. I veered in that direction.

Struggling fiercely against the tide and current, I swam toward that tiny spot of hope. Right when I felt as though I couldn't swim another stroke, my left foot brushed the top of a coral head. It was just wide enough for me to stand on and just shallow enough for my head and part of my shoulders to remain above the water.

I certainly must have been a peculiar sight; from a distance all anyone could see was this bloody pulp of a human head sticking out of the water in the middle of the ocean with absolutely nothing around it.

Chapter Five

Two fishermen from a nearby Sea Dayak village had been working the reef when our B-26 Marauder plunged into the ocean. They paddled their outrigger canoe toward the crash site as quickly as they possibly could. Man eating sharks infested the area around the reef and they'd soon be feasting on whatever they found in the water if they weren't doing so already.

The Dayaks of Borneo had great respect for anyone they thought to be English. Fortunately, they considered both Americans and Australians to be Englishmen, although of a lesser sort. The Dayak admiration for the English was primarily due to the fact that for decades, dozens of kindhearted western missionaries, most of them from England, had inundated Borneo in an attempt to convert the native peoples to Christianity. To a certain extent, these missionaries had been largely successful.

In addition to guiding the Dayak toward Christianity, the Englishmen also brought lifesaving medicines and food to the region and even helped build roads and schools for the local people.

Chapter Six

Because of the blood in my eyes and the rise and fall of the ocean swells, I couldn't really see the men inside the boat as they approached my perilous perch.

"Flyer, USA Flyer?" one of them called out.

I slowly lifted my right arm out of the water and motioned to them.

Thankfully they reached me a few minutes later and pulled me onto their outrigger canoe.

"I Kantu Kwi K and this my friend Batang Ulu," the small but muscular man said as he pointed to the man next to him.

Kantu Kwi K, who seemed to be only a little older than myself, sported two strange flower looking tattoos on the front of each shoulder. When he saw me looking at them, he smiled and pointed to the small black cross tattooed above my right wrist. He held up a tiny cross from the necklace he wore. "Me Jesus, too," he said.

I tried to speak but fell into unconsciousness. When I came to again, the men paid no attention to me but instead directed all their energy to the task of paddling the canoe. I sat up and tried to get my bearings. We were rapidly approaching a native village on the beach.

The outrigger part of the canoe caught a wave. Kantu Kwi K stopped paddling and turned the paddle into a rudder, deftly steering the canoe through the reef pass. He and his friend worked as a coordinated team, safely bringing us nearer to the beach second by second.

For all I knew, these men might be the legendary headhunters of Borneo and soon I might be their main course. However, as I sat in the wet bottom of the canoe, all I could do was stare up at the sky and grin.

Thank God I was alive.

If it was my fate to be boiled alive and eaten, I'd worry about that later. All I wanted to do right now was revel in the fact that I had survived.

Chapter Seven

I awoke sometime later, everything intact. I hadn't been abused but had, instead, been well tended to. Someone had bandaged my head with a cotton cloth and the cuts from the jagged reef had been cleaned and treated. My flight suit, pants, jacket, and worthless life preserver had been removed and now I wore little more than my skivvies.

I felt around my neck. My dog tags were missing. Head throbbing, I forced myself upright off of the thick pallet on the floor and began searching the room for my things. The one candle on a nearby crate did not give off enough light for me to see much beyond my own feet.

As I was about to try to leave the room, an old woman emerged from the darkness of the corner.

My heart pounded. Caretaker or guard?

Smiling, she gently held out a bowl.

"Tuak," she said, making drinking motions.

I took the bowl and sniffed the contents. An interesting, familiar odor filled my nose. Alcohol.

The door opened and in walked Kantu. "Good. You awake." He smiled. "You drink, tuak. Rice wine. It very good."

And it was.

"Where are my clothes and the rest of my gear?"

"We bury everything. If Japs find we die." He moved his index finger across his throat, stuck out his tongue, and made a gagging noise.

I nodded. "Okay. But I can't go around in my underwear." I snapped the skivvies away from my waist to show what I meant.

Kantu grinned and tossed something my way. "This *sarong* for you."

I frowned as I inspected what looked like a brightly patterned tablecloth. "A sarong? What's that?"

"You wrap this around your waist, like short pants."

After several unsuccessful attempts to cover myself, Kantu stepped in and wound the cloth just so and tucked it in here and there and, in no time, I was wearing my sarong. Thank God no one from home could see me. If Freddy were here, he'd never let me hear the end of it. It looked like I was wearing a big flowered diaper.

Apparently satisfied with my appearance, Kantu ushered me from the room intent on giving me a tour of the place. He called the structure a longhouse. Twenty doors ran from one end of the building to the other. Each led to someone's living quarters, called *biliks*.

A corridor, which was divided into three parts, ran the length of the building. The space in front of the door to each *bilik*, called the *tempuan,* belonged to whoever stayed in the *bilik* adjacent to it and was used as a workspace. The next part served as a public corridor from one end of the building to the other. The final space, the *pantai,* along the outer wall was reserved for guests.

I raised my brows and turned to Kantu. "I'm a guest, but you put me in a *bilik* instead of a *pantai*?"

He grinned. "That because you most honored guest. You deserve *bilik*. You Jap killer."

And I guess I was, or at least I had been when I'd been on bombing raids. Now *Betty Grable's Ass* sat at the bottom of the ocean and I was in a jungle crawling with Japanese soldiers. How long would it be before I came face to face with one of them? Would it be so easy then to kill?

I shuddered.

Kantu touched my arm. "What's wrong, Flyer. You in pain?"

In fact, my head still throbbed, but I brushed it off and encouraged Kantu to continue showing me around. Anything I learned about the Dayak might come in handy.

Kantu pointed out the *Ukirs*, or pictorial murals with tree and wild animal motifs, on the longhouse walls. He said that tribesmen with the decorating skills had created them as they had also created the highly decorated shields displayed near each bilik door. Human skulls, obtained during headhunting raids years earlier, also added to the decor.

A sudden image of the doomed Eddie Smith's face popped into my mind. How long before his head would look like these skulls? Nauseated now, I was relieved when Kantu ushered me outside, away from the gruesome relics.

The longhouse that we'd been in was just one of several built on raised stilts near a small river. Water buffalo, goats, and chickens sheltered themselves from the sun beneath each building.

As places went, this one wasn't so bad. Food seemed to be plentiful if my nose was to be trusted. The scent of roasting meat surrounded me.

I learned that dinner that evening would be in celebration of the first night of a festival called *Gawai Antu*, which in English translated roughly to, 'The Festival of the Dead.' I could only shake my head when I heard that. It was so all together fucking appropriate, after everything that I had experienced earlier in the day, that this, of course, would be the Dayak's festival of the dead.

I tried to stay occupied from one moment to the next in order to keep from thinking about the crash and the loss of my buddies, but by dinner time I was consumed with survivor's guilt and visions of Eddie's terrified face as he died.

As the sun began to set, I sat across a fire from Kantu and Batang, all of us enjoying the meal of fish and fruits and vegetables. I turned to Kantu. "Why did you and Batang risk your lives to save me?"

"Because you American and you hate Japs," Batang said.

Kantu explained by telling me about a missionary named John Willfinger whom the Dayak held in the highest regard. Thanks largely to his efforts and those of others like him, many of the Dayak were Christian and most could speak rudimentary English. He was revered by them.

When the Japs gained control of Borneo in 1942, they sent numerous patrols into the island's interior mountainous jungles searching for westerners who might be sponsoring subversive anti-Jap activities. Reverend Willfinger, not wanting his new Christian converts to have to lie about his whereabouts, turned himself in to the Japanese authorities.

The filthy Jap bastards beheaded him soon afterward. This singular barbaric act sent the Dayak into a fierce rage against the Japanese throughout Borneo.

Any enemy of the Japs was a friend of the Dayak.

It seemed that nearly everyone in the village was assembled in the village's central compound for the start of Gawai Antu. The villagers laughed and talked excitedly, most likely in anticipation of the night's activities, which Kantu had warned me were apt to get lively and were expected to last throughout most of the night, ending just before dawn.

Kantu pointed me toward a grass mat on the outer edge of the compound and told me to sit there. He brought me a cup of tuak and a bowl of rice smothered with something called sago worms.

I looked down at the squirming yellow larva and nearly puked.

Kantu grinned and patted my shoulder. "Eat, Flyer. Sago worms delicious and very good for you. You must eat them. They filled with protein and make you strong again."

I wasn't really convinced but couldn't see a way out of it. I slowly scooped up a squirmy pile of the sago worm rice mixture and stuffed it in my mouth.

Kantu had lied.

They were not delicious and my stomach started to heave, but I tried to keep my face neutral just as I had done when I'd received a shock from my Blue Bunny flight suit. My face turned red and tears welled in my eyes.

Kantu and Batang laughed hysterically at my obvious dissatisfaction with the Dayak delicacy.

Fine. I wouldn't puke in front of them and give them satisfaction. I took a long deep breath, and with my nostrils flared out, I forced myself to finish the entire dish. I ate every grain of rice and every last squiggly pus-filled worm.

When the villagers had finished their supper and had plied themselves silly with enormous amounts of *tuak* rice wine or *borak* rice beer, the village musicians began to play. The Ibans played tunes that in some ways sounded like traditional far eastern music. However their use of brass gongs and drums gave their music a distinctly unique sound. Kantu called this strange amalgam of instruments *agung* ensembles. It was certainly interesting.

"When did the Iban musicians start using guitars in their music?" I asked Kantu as I pointed at the instrument in question.

"That not guitar, Flyer. It a *sape*." He informed me that the *sape* was a traditional Iban instrument and had been used for as long as he could remember.

Still looked a lot like a guitar to me.

The steady rhythm of the *sape*, drum, and gong music created music that sounded like a blend of Irish and Japanese folk music. The haunting tunes, along with the rice wine, helped me relax for the first time since the crash. I had almost started to drift off to sleep when a dozen costumed warriors ran out of the nearby jungle and jumped directly into the middle of the ceremony.

My eyes opened wide and Kantu jumped up. "Flyer, whatever you do, don't touch the warrior dancers!"

"Why?"

"They will chop off your head and shrink it to the size of a grapefruit!" He began mimicking the slow spinning, bowing, and twisting dance moves of the *Hivan Kayo* warriors.

I quickly pulled my arms and legs inward, as close to my body as possible. No way did I want to accidently touch anyone. I was so tightly coiled up I felt like I was hugging myself from the inside out.

The dancing warriors, covered with tattoos from head to toe, wore elaborate masks decorated with what looked like human hair, skin, and teeth. The eyes and lips of the masks were bold and overly exaggerated. The headdress of one of the dancers consisted of a magnificent plume of colored feathers taken from the exotic jungle birds. I was awed, impressed, and scared shitless by the warriors as they performed the traditional opening dance. I watched intently as the last warrior in the *Ngajat*, which was what Batang called this traditional Iban festival dance, came into the circle. He hoisted a strangely decorated black bag above his head.

As the *Taboh* and *Geudang* music reached its grand crescendo in a cacophony of smashing drums and banging gongs, the warrior reached deep into the ornate black bag. His arm lingered inside for a moment and then, without warning, he whipped out two human heads and held them high for all to see.

The crowd shrieked with joy.

"Those heads over one hundred years old," Batang whispered near my ear.

All of the skin had been removed and they had been boiled, cleaned, and shrunken to the exact size of, you guessed it, a grapefruit.

I had never seen such a gruesome sight and yet couldn't take my eyes away from it.

The warrior then stowed the heads back in the bag and the dance ended.

I was contemplating another bowl of *Tuak* followed by a long night's sleep, when Kantu rushed to me and Batang. "Flyer, we have to leave soon," he said. "Jungle runners say Jap bastards coming soon." He held up two fingers.

I bolted upright. "When, two hours, two minutes, two seconds?"

"Days," Kantu said. "Takes long time to move in jungle. They looking for Americans."

I looked out into the distance, at the dark jungle that bordered one side of the village. "I'll go now."

Kantu grabbed my shoulder as I was turning to walk away. "Not now. You need plan, supplies, and help. Take time for all that. We be long gone before Japs. No worry." He grinned at me and squeezed my shoulder.

"We?"

"Batang and me, we take you to Z-force. They help you."

In order to survive, I would once again have to relinquish control of my life to others, to people who didn't know me or owe me anything.

"Where are we going?" I asked Kantu.

"Into the interior Apokayan Highlands, far away from coast. Z-force in the mountains."

I had heard talk of Z-force, aka Z unit but never imagined that my life would depend on us finding them.

Z-force was an allied commando outfit that had been operating in central Borneo since mid-1942. Comprised primarily of Australians and Brits and allied

Borneo headhunters, their mission was to sabotage Jap installations, provide reconnaissance for the impending Allied invasion of Borneo, and to search for and assist downed Allied pilots while killing as many Japs as possible along the way.

"We sleep now, pack tomorrow then leave."

Who was I to argue? Kantu was the man with the plan.

I gulped down the last of my rice wine and went to sleep.

Kantu, Batang, and I arose before sunrise. Though my head throbbed, I set about helping them pack supplies for our trek. By mid-morning we had finished our preparations and were ready to leave.

Kantu and Batang said tearful goodbyes to their family members. Although their journey would only last a few weeks at best, everyone involved knew how dangerous it was. Kantu and Batang pulled their primitive backpacks onto their shoulders. They carried large Iban machetes in their packs and each of them held onto long blow pipes, which were used to shoot poisonous darts at their enemies. I was given a smaller backpack and machete but no blowpipe. Good thing, probably, since I didn't have a clue in the world how to load the dart without getting poison on myself.

I still had no shirt other than my undershirt and still wore my sarong shorts. Since the villagers had seen fit to bury my boots along with the rest of my uniform, Kantu's father gave me a pair of his shoes to wear on the journey. He called them thongs, and unfortunately they really only protected the bottoms of my feet.

Batang's father plopped a large woven hat on my head. "Sun bad, shade good," he said with a smile. Aside from my lighter skin and much shorter hair, I looked almost identical to Kantu and Batang.

We had enough supplies to make it to the nearby village of Sibu. We would restock as best as possible when we got there. After that food was used up, we intended to forage for anything else we needed for survival. We would be totally dependent on the land and on Kantu and Batang's ability to get us what we needed. This inevitability seemingly caused no anxiety whatsoever among Kantu and Batang, but I was greatly concerned. I was kind of fond of eating things other than sago worms and other nasty creeping, crawling, and or flying bugs.

Our general plan was fairly simple and straightforward.

Kantu laid it out for me as we started the trek. We would take the coastal path southwest from the village, which was located just south of Bintulu, to the Rajang river mouth, just beyond the village of Mukah. Approximately a twenty-five-mile trip. Once at the river mouth, we would procure a small canoe and proceed a few more miles upriver to the village of Sibu. After resupplying there, we would continue on via boat, to the village of Kapit near the junction of the Rajang and Baleh Rivers. Once we arrived at the foothills of the mountainous interior, we would abandon our boat and proceed through the jungle on foot.

I looked at Kantu and grinned. "Did you say 'abandon our boat' or 'abandon all hope'?"

Both men just stared at me and remained silent.

"Get it," I said, "abandon all hope? From Dante's Divine Comedy, right before he enters into hell?"

More blank stares and deafening silence greeted my failed attempt at humor.

"Okay, guys, forget it," I said. "What do we do after we abandon the boat?"

Kantu shrugged. "The last part of journey, we climb the highlands until we reached Mount Bawoei. That's where we'll find Z-force." Kantu had heard through the Dayak grapevine that Z-force was building a crude airstrip on top of Mt. Bawoei in hopes of flying in supplies and flying out rescued allied flyers shot down in the area.

He'd also heard that this particular Special Forces unit was headed by an eccentric British anthropologist named Tom Harrisson, who, during the early 1930s, had spent many years studying the indigenous tribes of Borneo. He was quite the character, a white westerner covered with Dayak tattoos. He blended in with the locals with such ease and gracefulness that he seemed to be one of them. He knew everything there was to know about the Kelabit and Lun Dayeh cultures. He knew their languages and their general histories, but most importantly he knew that they hated the Japs and craved revenge for the murder of Reverend Willfinger and various other Christian missionaries.

He'd trained hundreds of Borneo men in the art of guerilla warfare and encouraged local tribesmen to bring back the age old custom of headhunting, something that I knew had been officially banned for nearly one hundred years.

Historically headhunting had been an integral part of life in Borneo since its earliest origins. Most often it was used for the obvious reason—revenge, but it also played an important societal role with regard to spiritual cleansing and cosmic balance. It was an incredibly violent and horrific act that carried significant meaning and symbolism among the indigenous peoples of Borneo. Knowing this all too well, Harrisson apparently had tapped into it and employed it against the Japs.

I just hoped the headhunters didn't mistake my head for one that needed to be shrunken.

For the next few hours, as we trudged toward Z-force, I couldn't stop thinking about the headhunters or the shrunken heads I'd seen the previous evening.

The coastal trail toward the river mouth was a narrow pathway comprised mainly of sand and flat volcanic rock. The trail meandered southward, sandwiched between the warm, blue ocean on my right and the lush, green jungle on my left.

Despite the fact that we traveled near the ocean, the day was an absolute scorcher, without much of a breeze. As Kantu and Batang seemed to walk effortlessly, sweat poured from my forehead directly into my eyes, irritating them to no end. My head still ached from the violent impact of the crash and, no doubt, from the large portion of rice wine I'd gulped down. In fact, my sweat reeked of booze and seemed to attract every biting and stinging insect in the area.

My spirits, however, were buoyed the farther away we moved from Kantu and Batang's village. The Japs undoubtedly were closing in on the village and it was going to take a Herculean effort to stay one step ahead of them. But I had no doubt that we would do it. We had to.

Batang and Kantu and their people had saved my life. I prayed often that their assistance would never be revealed. And chances were good that the Japs would never suspect that I'd been there. All evidence of my stay in the village had been removed. I had simply disappeared without a trace. At least I hoped so.

Because I was an aviator or "Flyer" as Kantu and Batang called me, I had often been briefed by Bomber Command about the overall concentration of Japanese troops on the island of Borneo. An estimate of Japanese troop strength on the island was presumed to be at about thirty five thousand. We were headed southwest, toward the Mukah/Sibu area, populated by at least two thousand Japs around the town of Kuching. In addition to these troops, it was also widely believed that there was a large Allied POW camp in region.

I tried not to dwell on the negatives and the implausibility of eluding the Japs and effecting an extraction of myself off of this island. Instead, I

concentrated, for a while, on putting one foot in front of the

other without falling down from heat stroke or exhaustion.

Chapter Eight

Just like clockwork a Japanese patrol showed up at Kantu's village the next day. Kantu's father and the other village elders were rounded up and interrogated. They, of course, denied knowing anything about the American plane that had been shot down near the village.

Kantu's father attempted to convince the Japs that the entire crew had most likely perished in the ocean. Meanwhile, during the two-hour interrogation, Jap soldiers rifled through every single room, in every single longhouse, looking for evidence that the villagers might be lying.

Everyone in the village was on edge, both the Dayak and the Japs.

After a few hours of intense scouring, one of the Japanese soldiers pointed to an area at the edge of the village, just inside the jungle canopy. The ground seemed freshly disturbed and wasn't covered with the same amount of leaves and brush as the surrounding jungle floor.

Suspicious, he and a couple of other soldiers set about digging. One of the soldiers bent down and picked up something, then shouted. He jogged over to the Major and dropped something into his palm.

The major's face filled with rage. Eyes piercing, he drew in a deep breath and called out for Kantu's father and the other village elders. The elder chiefs quickly appeared, approaching the Major with their heads bowed slightly.

"Tie them up," the major yelled to his men. "Hands behind their backs." Within minutes, amidst the wails of the village women and children, half a dozen of the old men were bound with leather straps, arms squeezed much too tightly against their bodies.

The major held up the object for all the villagers to see. "What is this?" he shouted.

People close enough to see it moaned and several of them stepped back, as if moving away from the object would somehow absolve them from any danger that its presence posed.

"How did these American dog tags get here?" the major said through clenched teeth.

No one spoke.

He asked again.

Still no one spoke.

He untied two of the men and pulled them out of the group. "Down on your knees!" he screamed into their faces, spit flying, as he pushed down on the shoulders of one of them.

"This is your last chance. Where are the Americans? How many are there? Talk!"

The only sound came from the waves crashing on the distant reef and the wind rushing through the palm trees.

Kantu's father and three other village elders were beheaded that day.

The fury and barbarism of the Japanese soldiers would surely have continued if it hadn't been for the actions of a scared, little girl. She stepped out of the crowd, held up her tiny trembling index finger and pointed toward the jungle. South towards Sibu the Japs figured.

Chapter Nine

We averaged about ten to twelve miles per day, walking along the beach trail. Even though I was exhausted at the end of each day, I still had trouble sleeping. I couldn't stop thinking of my dead buddies resting on the bottom of the South China Sea. I replayed the crash—what I could remember of it—over and over in a loop in my head, always wondering why I had survived and they hadn't.

Fear of Jap patrols also kept me on edge. On the morning of the second day, as the sky lightened and the darkness retreated to its proper hiding place, I felt the tension lift from my body, tension that had been spawned by my fear of the dark, unknown world that I was now trying to survive in. Now that it was light outside, I could at least see what was coming—and I had no doubt that something was definitely coming.

During the late afternoon of that same day, the three of us finally completed the twenty-five-mile journey from Kantu's village to the mouth of the Rajang River. I was already beginning to dread the coming of nightfall and was anxious to keep moving and find some place safe to bed down.

The few huts near the river mouth seemed abandoned. The place was quiet, way too quiet. It was eerie. The usual jungle sounds seemed diminished. Neither Kantu nor Batang seemed concerned. Observing their composure, I told myself to relax and stay focused.

"What now, guys," I said. "Where's the boat?"

"It's not here," said Kantu.

Well, I could see that. Before I could ask what we were going to do next, Batang and Kantu started walking again, this time along the river's edge. We still seemed to be heading south, toward Sibu.

After a few hours of rest, we got up before dawn and began moving once again toward Sibu. Our speed had slowed considerably as the river trail was muddy and filled with blood sucking leeches that we had to pull off our skin every few minutes.

For much of the trek we actually walked in the shallow part of the water, which at certain times seemed easier to traverse than the rivers muddy edge. About halfway to Sibu, Batang suddenly raised his hand and stopped walking. He put his finger to his lips, motioning for us to be silent. Kantu and I followed his lead.

He eventually lowered his arm. As he did so, an eleven foot python slithered directly in front of him, its massive head jutting out, just above the waterline. A second later, it passed directly between his legs.

Trying to remain stoic in front of Kantu and Batang, I fought the urge to shriek.

When the snake had disappeared behind us, Batang looked at Kantu, raised his eyebrows, and grinned. Humor was the last thing on my mind, but I forced myself to mimic the look. I did not want to lose the respect of these men who were putting their lives on the line for me.

A couple of hours later, we reached the outskirts of Sibu. "Wait here," Kantu said. "Batang and I will get supplies and a boat."

"You want me to stay here alone?" I frowned as I pulled another leach from my calf.

Kantu reached into Batang's backpack and started pulling things out of it. "I'll keep these for us," he said "and these, too, the rest stays with you." He left their blowpipes with me as well. Kantu thought that possession of tightly stuffed traveling packs and weapons would only arouse suspicion.

As usual, he was probably right.

"Find a place to hide. We be back soon." Kantu and Batang strode away without looking back.

I found a cloistered area on the left side of the riverbank that provided exceptional coverage and hid there.

I didn't feel any better with the weapons Kantu had left with me. I'd never used a blowpipe and the odds that I could hit anything with a tiny dart were slim to none.

An hour after Kantu and Batang left me alone I had to take a piss, though I was loath to move from my hiding spot.

I had been sitting for so long and my muscles had been so tensed and tightly coiled in expectation of sudden discovery that, when I finally stood up, my feet tingled with pins and needles. I squeezed my toes and rubbed my legs, trying to restore the circulation faster. I really needed to pee but didn't want to chance stumbling about and hurting myself.

After the tingling and numbness abated, I turned around, facing the tree on which I planned to water.

My heart jumped into my throat.

Two incredibly fierce looking headhunters stood directly behind me.

They had appeared suddenly and swiftly, unseen and unheard like ghosts from the jungle. A sense of unreality overcame me—that I should find myself in such dire circumstances, lost on an island, in the middle of nowhere, facing death at the hands savages when I'd already managed to elude the Jap beasts at least twice, well it just didn't seem fair. I could almost believe that I had somehow fallen into a nightmare without first falling asleep.

Without really thinking, I reached for my machete.

In perfect synchronicity with my movement, one of the warriors lifted his poisonous blowpipe to his lips and pointed it at me. The other waved his *Mandau* at me and slowly shook his head from side to side.

I had no choice but to lower my weapon. A second later, the tribesman with the blowpipe lowered his weapon away from his mouth.

He smiled ever so slightly and nodded. Apparently, they were in no hurry to kill me.

At that moment the sound of Japanese voices reached me.

The Dayak warriors, using hand gestures, instructed me to follow them away from the river. I seemed to have no other option, the lesser of two evils feeling like the safer choice at the moment.

I picked up the equipment Kantu and Batang had left behind and the three of us quickly got the hell out of there.

Once we climbed the foothills along the river and found a safer vantage point, we looked back to reconnoiter the situation below. Two dozen Japs patrolled the area. They didn't seem to be searching for anything in particular. Rather, they seemed to be meandering along. It was probably just a routine patrol along the river. Still I felt unnerved. This was the closest I'd ever been to Jap soldiers.

After the enemy patrol moved on, the Dayak warriors relocated me to an even safer place—an abandoned longhouse, still outside of the village but on its other side. The warrior who seemed to be in charge pointed at my three backpacks and two blowpipes. He tilted his head slightly to the right and inquiringly held up two fingers.

I nodded, trying to let him know that I was traveling with two allies. I pointed toward the village. Who knew if my gestures had translated into a reliable message?

But I worried what would happen if Kantu and Batang didn't find me at the river hideout? Might they do something drastic and get themselves killed?

Seemingly understanding my concern the warriors squatted down and began to talk among themselves. Soon thereafter, one of the warriors left. The leader put his hand on my shoulder, as if to reassure me that everything would be okay.

But would it be?

They hid me beneath a false floor, in one of the *biliks*. They were obviously taking no chances.

A few hours later, the Dayak warrior returned with Kantu and Batang. After being freed from my place of sequestration, I leapt up and group-hugged Batang and then Kantu. Apparently not knowing how to respond, they merely smiled, arms remaining firmly at their sides. Even when it dawned on me that Kantu and Batang might be uncomfortable with my unexpected outburst of physical affection, I still couldn't bring myself to release them. I was so damned happy they were okay.

When I finally broke off the long heartfelt embrace, Kantu quickly stepped away from me to a much safer distance and began to explain what had happened. The warriors who'd just saved me from the Jap patrol had been tracking us since we'd come across the snake in the river. They'd been cautious about approaching us until they found out who we were and what our intentions were.

Kantu and Batang had been aware of their presence for a while, but hadn't bothered to tell me because they didn't want to frighten me anymore than I already was. However, after they set off by themselves, they felt the time was right to make contact. They told the tracking warriors about me and asked that they keep a watch over me while they were gone.

When the warriors saw the Jap patrol in the vicinity they acted immediately and secreted me away from the enemy.

Amazing. Here was another group of complete strangers who'd risked their lives for me. Who was I to deserve such selflessness?

That night we all slept in the abandoned longhouse. The Dayak warriors took turns as night watchman in case any Japs came sniffing around. We arose early the next morning and set about planning how we could safely proceed to Kapit.

It was decided that I would travel slightly eastward with the two Dayak warriors along the village trail. Dressed as a local Iban, I would wear my large woven hat pulled down over my face, like so many of the indigenous people did.

Kantu and Batang would take a small canoe they had borrowed from one of the villagers and proceed eastward via the river. About ten miles on the other side of Sibu, we would regroup.

From there Kantu, Batang and I would continue in the boat and the Dayak warriors would return to the jungle.

Incredibly, it worked out exactly as planned. There were with no hitches.

Once we were safely on the eastern side of Sibu and well outside of the routine Japanese patrol area, we said goodbye to our two Dayak friends. They had been of tremendous assistance to us. They gave Kantu a crudely drawn map and indicated on it where we could expect Jap checkpoints along the river. They emptied their packs of dried fruit and Sago worms and offered them to us for our journey.

Never in my life had I encountered such kind people. Surely I had been blessed when Kantu and Batang had plucked me out of the ocean and later when the two Ibans had rescued me from imminent Japanese capture. How could I ever possibly begin to repay them or the other generous natives of Borneo?

Maybe I could start by killing some Japs.

Once safely in the canoe, I turned to wave a final goodbye to my new found warrior friends but they had already disappeared back into the dense green jungle from where they had come. I'd not even asked them their names.

The river trip was slow going. We had to paddle and use poles much of the time. The water was bright yellow and seemed to be teaming with fish and other wildlife. It was indeed a surreal feeling as we slowly floated through the intensely vivid green jungle on a golden watery path knowing that at any moment I could be killed or taken prisoner. The range of emotions raging inside of me changed often from acute anxiety to a spiritual calm then back to anxiety in the blink of an eye.

On those occasions when we came upon Japanese checkpoints Kantu and I disembarked from the canoe and let Batang pilot it alone. Kantu and I went up and around the Jap soldiers via the foothills. Then we reunited on the other side of the checkpoint. We wasted a lot of time doing this, but it was the only safe way to pass them and thus, became a part of our routine. So far, we had successfully avoided any detection whatsoever by the numerous Jap patrols along the river, and we planned to keep it that way.

After traveling for a few days, we arrived at the village of Kanawit. We approached the tiny settlement with great caution. Though we didn't think that it was a Jap checkpoint trap, we weren't about to take any chances. Kanawit was an important destination for us as it was the last village where we could get supplies before our final push toward to Kapit.

Kantu and I waited for Batang on the eastern outskirts of Kanawit. When he finally showed up a few hours later, he had uncovered some useful information. One of the villagers informed him that the Japs had confirmed that one or more Americans had survived a plane crash and that he, with the aid of Dayak natives, were making their way toward Sibu.

"Shit," I said. "So much for flying under the Jap's radar. It's a wonder we haven't already been captured."

Batang nodded. "You not only thorn in Japs' side, Flyer. They also looking extra hard for any sign of Z-force."

Apparently, according to Batang's source, a lone member of Z-force was conducting daily sabotage operations in the Kapit region. And a week earlier this same Z-force commando had ventured into one of the remote, outlying village longhouses searching for medicine to help one of his Dayak accomplices fight the Beriberi.

No one, however, had seen the mysterious white man since then.

Although I had only been in Borneo for a few weeks and the news Batang brought was bad, talk of another white man made my heart soar. Maybe the commando could help get me off of this island.

Excitedly, I tried to hurry Kantu and Batang along. Our plan was to continue in the canoe until we reached Kapit. After we reached the village, we would hide our canoe and follow the river east on foot, until it turned south at the base of the highland's foothills. At that point we would start our slow ascent toward Mount Bawoei and freedom.

The journey from Kanawit to Kapit was roughly one hundred and twenty five miles. Since traveling by canoe down the Japanese infested Rajang River over such a long distance would be painfully slow and extremely dangerous, especially now that we knew that the Japs knew about me, we came up with a contingency plan. Actually, they came up with the plan and I just listened.

In a scene straight out of Joseph Conrad's epic *Heart of Darkness*, they concocted a new "riverboat" strategy. We would take the old Belgian steamboat *Roi des Belges* to our final destination.

Before our new scheme could be set in motion, we had to determine who outside of our little group could be trusted. It was obvious that most Dayaks in the region hated the Japs and wanted the Allies to expel them from Borneo. However, some Dayaks were self-serving and most assuredly would sell us out if the price was right.

Given that we were so far from Kantu and Batang's village, they had little idea about whom they could trust. Unfortunately, we didn't have many options and time was of the essence. Fueled on by the apparent disloyalty of the locals now assisting me and men of Z-force, I was quite certain that the Japs would leave no stone unturned in trying to find us.

Kantu thought that he and Batang should reconnoiter the steamboat and its crew to see if it would be safe enough for us to use. After spending time at the docks, they found a potential ally to assist us, the ship's first mate, Kelander Miller.

Kela, as he was called, was the son of an English missionary named William Miller and his Iban wife, Dorat. His father, who had recently died from Malaria, had been a popular Christian missionary in the region. Since the brutal Japanese invasion of China in 1937, Pastor Miller had constantly railed against Japanese imperialism.

Kela had been greatly influenced by his father's noble work. In fact, he had participated in helping local Iban saboteurs disrupt Japanese communications in the region on two separate occasions, and, of even greater importance, he had personally assassinated three high ranking Japanese government officials in the area. His actions were so cloaked in secrecy that even his own family members didn't know about them. Batang and Kantu were certain that Kela Miller could be trusted.

How my Dayak friends had gathered this information, they never said, not even to me. I respected their sense of loyalty. Their unassailable honor confirmed to me absolutely and without question, that my presence in Borneo would never ever be revealed to anyone by either of these noble men, even under the most dire and distressing circumstances.

Chapter Ten

The steamboat *Roi des Belges* consisted of two levels.

The bottom section was divided equally between an open air sitting area filled with old wooden benches and a sheltered sleeping area containing rope hammocks and rattan floor mats. A crude toilet space at the very back of the sleeping area consisted of a wooden platform seat with a hole cut in its center. Human waste fell through the hole, directly into the river. The only thing separating the sleeping space from the shitting place was a rickety bamboo door that didn't shut completely.

The Captain's wheelhouse and two tiny bedrooms for the Captain and the first mate comprised the entirety of the top level. The roof of the wheelhouse was completely flat and the only thing up there was a painted wooden flagpole, which always flew the Japanese rising sun. At the very back of the flat roof was a storage area that had been cut out of the roof. About the size of a coffin, it was maybe seven feet long, two feet wide, and twenty inches deep.

Kela thought that I could be stowed away in the space during the daylight hours. At night, under the cover of darkness, he suggested that I could cautiously come out of my steamboat sarcophagus and stretch out on the cool roof. He would sneak food and water to me throughout the weeklong trip.

Since it was part of Kela's daily routine to go up to the storage bin to retrieve things no one would suspect anything. However, for the plan to work, storage goods would have to be secretly relocated from the rooftop storage bin into Kela's miniscule bedroom, making the already small area much more cramped.

Lastly, if a Japanese patrol boat suddenly approached, Kela would sound the ship's horn in two short but distinct bursts to notify me of the situation. Kela sternly warned me that if I ever heard the horns bellow, I was to jump off the roof and into the river without hesitation.

He told me to swim to the shoreline and find a hiding spot. He would immediately mark this area on his navigation charts and Kantu and Batang would later return to retrieve me. Needless to say, I didn't feel very confident about this plan but knew that I didn't have much of a choice. I would just have to make the best of a bad situation. That was, if I could even get on the ship.

My boarding it presented a huge problem. I couldn't just walk on, even disguised as a local Dayak. Japanese soldiers often used the *Roi des Belges* to get from Sibu to Kapit, especially when they were on leave.

We were about to give up on our plan to steal a ride on the steamboat when Kela suggested that Kantu take me east along the river until we reached the Brooke Forest Bridge, a low hanging, rope and wood plank, suspension bridge, about two miles on the other side of Kanawit. Kantu would return and board the steamboat with Batang.

I would have to remain hidden along the riverbank until I saw the *Roi des Belges* coming down the river. With Kela at the helm, he would slow the ship to a crawl as it passed underneath the bridge. At that exact moment, I would simply walk out onto the bridge, throw myself over its side, drop on top of the ship's roof then scramble to my predetermined safe place.

The plan sounded easy enough and seemed quite plausible.

It also sounded scary as hell for me.

Kela had already provided Kantu and Batang with tickets and enough food to last through the voyage. The *Rois des Belges* was scheduled to depart for Kapit around seven that evening. The timing couldn't have been any better. Since it would be nearly dark by the time that the boat passed under the bridge, I would have a great opportunity to get onboard without being noticed.

Shortly after noon, Kantu and I left for the bridge, rain steadily pouring from the sky. Though uncomfortable to travel in, the rain allowed me to pull my broad hat completely over my head, lessening my chance of detection. All of our packs and equipment had been left with Batang to be taken on the boat later when he and Kantu boarded. The only thing Kantu and I carried were our machetes. The path on which we slogged had transformed into a soupy mess of mud and muck.

It took us a couple of hours to reach Kanawit. At the village's outskirts, a severe bend in the trail gave us a moment of pause. We couldn't see anything beyond the curve and neither of us fancied walking into a surprise.

An hour passed before we convinced ourselves that we had no alternative but to continue around the curve and into the village. As we rounded the corner, our good luck ran out. A Japanese checkpoint stood directly in front of us.

My heart raced and I was considering whether or not I should break into a backward sprint.

Kantu casually leaned close. "Easy, Flyer," he whispered.

I took a long, deep breath and looked up ever so slightly. Three Jap guards sat in a crudely-constructed wooden shed, smoking cigarettes. One of them glanced directly at us and then looked away.

I was so scared that I farted. I couldn't help it, it just came flying out of my ass completely unannounced. Kind of like when you sneeze but accidently fart too.

Kantu chuckled as we resumed walking along the trail, past the guard post, to our rendezvous.

It took us another half an hour to reach the suspension bridge on the other side of the village. When no one was around Kantu and I simply stepped off the trail and melted into the rain soaked jungle.

We found an excellent spot to hide in a small indentation along the side of a hill near the bridge. It wasn't quite a cave but almost. Huge green leaves from a nearby banana and rubber trees hung low over the top of the indentation. This provided us with shelter and a fairly dry space in which to secret ourselves.

Kantu climbed a nearby tree and retrieved a bunch of bananas for me to eat. He showed me how to bend one of the big banana leaves in order to funnel rainwater into my mouth. After a few minutes, apparently satisfied that I was safe, fed, and watered enough for the time being, Kantu nodded slightly and smiled.

I stuck out my hand. "Goodbye friend, I'll see you soon."

He stared at my hand and then finally shook it. "Okay, Flyer. Be safe."

A second later he was gone.

After an hour, the rain stopped and the clouds broke up. As the sun dropped lower in the late afternoon sky, I became more focused on what I had to do. I carefully monitored the bridge from my hideout, observing the patterns of local foot traffic. Surprisingly, there was a lot of it. I also scanned the river for approaching river craft, Jap or civilian.

The Japs at the checkpoint worried me. I half expected to see one or more of them appear at any moment, searching for the farting Yankee in the floppy hat. And even if that didn't happen, I was worried that one of the Japs might see me when I walked out onto the bridge.

Fortunately, because the Rajang River basically followed the same meandering route that the village path did, the Japs probably didn't have a clear view of the suspension bridge from their guard post. At least I hoped they didn't.

Although the bridge looked dilapidated, it seemed fairly sturdy still when people walked across it. It certainly bounced and swayed a bit, but overall it probably would last through my time when I had to leap from it. The bridge's handrail was simply a two inch thick rope.

It seemed like the best way for me to get onto the boat would be to lay down on the wooden boards and dangle myself over the side. Then, when the *Roi des Belges* passed below, I would simply drop down onto it.

During that strange part of the day, late in the afternoon, at a time poets often refer to as the gloaming, when it looks like the sun didn't even know if it was rising or setting and everything in the world seemed enveloped in peculiar tone of greyish blue sepia, I fell asleep. For some inexplicable reason, at that very moment, I felt incredibly safe in my jungle sanctuary.

I must have been really exhausted because I did something that I never do. I had a dream. I was in a big, old, wooden house looking out the window. It was freezing outside and fresh snow covered the ground. Icicles dripped from the edge of the roof like frozen stalactites. The clouds were dark and gray, heavy and low, yet tiny slivers of magnificent bright red and orange streaks peeked out from beneath them, just above the edge of the horizon, where the sun was setting.

A terrific snowstorm had just passed and clear weather was ahead. A mysterious and beautiful dark-haired woman whom I did not recognize and who was dressed as if she was from the mid-nineteenth century appeared before me.

"The war is over, our side has won," she whispered.

I walked outside, into the bitterly cold air and took a deep breath. My lungs burned at the infusion of icy air. I silently stared at the bare, black trees in the distance, snow drifts creeping up their trunks, their branches drooping low from the weight upon them.

Near the grove of trees was a small grave with a marble headstone. An enormous sense of doom came over me.

The mysterious woman now stood beside me on the front porch. "Yes, Alex, it's yours," she said, "But not yet. You still have much work to do." She turned to me and opened up her mouth widely as if to scream, but nothing came out except a loud blast.

The loud blast startled me awake.

My eyes opened even wider with the second blast of the horn. Kela and the *Roi des Belges* were rounding the bend of the river. I rubbed my eyes and slapped at my cheeks as I quickly ran toward the bridge.

Kela seemed to be approaching the bridge way too fast.

I grabbed the rope handrail and scurried out onto the middle of the bridge. I tried to position myself in a straight line with the fast approaching steamboat. Out of the corner of my eye I saw two old men walking onto the bridge from the other side. They were dressed like 'friendlies,' but I couldn't be sure. As the locals came closer, I lay down on my stomach and grabbed the rope running alongside of the bottom part of the bridge.

It seemed now as if Kela had slowed the boat almost to a complete stop.

I rolled off the side of the bridge and, instead of dropping onto the boat's roof, I simply dangled there for a few seconds.

The top of the boat was much lower than I had I thought it would be; it had to be at least fifteen feet below me.

Shit.

My hands burned from gripping the rope so tightly. It was now or never.

"Lord have mercy," I mumbled to myself. I let go and fell for what seemed like an eternity.

My back slammed onto the roof with a hard thud. I gasped for air in that panicked state that every school boy knows all too well, the wind completely knocked out of me.

As I stared up at the sky, wondering if my ribs and spine were broken, the faces of the two old men on the bridge slowly came into focus. One of the men smiled at me and gave me the thumbs up sign.

Although in severe pain, I lifted my injured right hand and signaled him back as the *Roi des Belges* slowly drifted underneath the rickety old suspension bridge.

Once I regained my breath I rolled onto my stomach. Eventually when I looked back at the men on the bridge, they were already on the other side.

I was attempting to get to my knees when I heard a voice in the distance.

Kantu's head appeared, just barely visible above the roofline at the other end of the ship. He signaled for me to hurry up and get into my safe spot. I quickly crawled to the far end of the roof. When I got to my tiny little tomb I pulled the door aside just enough for me to drop into the space below.

I laid on my back and slowly secured the door into place. It was a scene that could have been straight out of some bizarre jungle adaptation of *Nosferatu*, but at least for the moment I was safe.

Because it was now completely dark outside, I wasn't able to see the water and fruit Kela had left for me at the other end of the box. Even though it was somewhat cooler outside due to the earlier rainstorm, the inside of the box was stifling. Nevertheless, I thought it best to stay concealed for at least a couple of hours before I ventured back outside.

Using a left behind chunk of a mildewed orange life jacket as a pillow, I tried to get comfortable. I took a few deep breaths and shut my eyes. Sleep however, eluded me. I was hot and riddled with anxiety.

I cracked the door above me ever so slightly to let in the fresh breeze outside. I could hear the repetitive cadence of the steamboat's engines below me. *Cachunk, cachunk, cachunk.* The water pouring off of the massive paddlewheel sounded like a cascading waterfall.

I imagined I was skinny dipping with a beautiful Sheila back in Australia—something I had yet to experience. The mesmerizing rhythm of the mechanized metronome soothed me until I finally slipped into a deep sleep.

I slept soundly for a few hours. Feeling nature's call, I carefully pushed the already cracked door above me farther to the side. My white hand thrust into the dark night as if it were coming out of the grave of some Bela Lugosi vampire flick. I looked out over the edge of my hiding spot, scanning the entire roof from bow to stern. The coast seemed to be clear for Operation: Take-A-Piss.

As quietly as I could, I pulled myself out and up onto the roof, then crept toward the edge of the roof. After I'd peed off the side of the boat, I retraced my steps to my hiding spot. But before I got back in, I decided to lie on the roof for a while. It felt so nice and cool on my back, I didn't want to return to the pit of hell.

An amazing assortment of stars filled up every inch of the blackness above me. Because of the absence of any light in the jungle, the stars in Borneo looked especially vivid. As I stared at the heavens, I thought about my dad. Before he'd abandoned us, he'd built a planetarium of sorts in my bedroom.

He'd positioned a light bulb underneath a big box into which he'd punched tiny holes in the form of a few of the major constellations. With the room lights off and the flashlight on, he and I reclined together on my bed and stared at the star-projected ceiling while talking about the stars. We both agreed that the Big Dipper was our favorite constellation.

Now, on top of the *Rois des Belges,* I searched the night sky until I located the Big Dipper. I remembered that Dusty Purdy, the now deceased navigator on *Betty Grable's Ass*, had once told me that the people of Borneo and Indonesia called the Big Dipper *Buruj Biduk*. I soon fell asleep, comforted by happy and peaceful thoughts of my dad and Dusty and *Buruj Biduk*.

Chapter Eleven

The doctor's incredibly bright headlamp shined right into my eyes, stinging them.

I raised my hand and tried to shield myself from the light. "Do my tonsils have to come out?" I asked the doctor in a voice that I hadn't heard in years.

"I'm afraid so, Alex. But don't worry. Afterward, you'll get to eat lots and lots of delicious ice cream."

A dish of ice cream appeared before me, but it melted to soup in an instant.

The sun's incredibly bright presence shined through my eyelids.

Oh, my God, I'd fallen asleep on the roof and it was now broad daylight!

How long had I been stretched out on top of the *Rois des Belges*? Had anyone seen me? How could I have made such a mistake?

I rolled over and threw myself into the shallow pit and quickly pulled the door closed. I was breathing heavily and sweating like a pig, but I dare not move. After what felt like an hour, when no one had come to rip me from my hiding spot and kill me, I cracked the door a tiny bit to let in some fresh air. Although it couldn't have been much past 10:00 o'clock in the morning—the sun wasn't yet quite overhead—my tiny tomb was already boiling hot. How in the hell was I going to survive in there until nightfall?

My first full day in the box was a complete nightmare. I was burning up, desperate for more water and had to take a fierce dump, maybe even the dump of a lifetime. There is absolutely no worse feeling than having to take a crap and not being able to.

Shortly after midday, footsteps sounded on the ladder. I quickly secured the door above me.

A minute later the door was yanked violently to the side.

Kela didn't smile or say a word. He merely dropped more food and water into the pit, closed the door, then left.

I didn't have enough room to sit up and drink the water so I pushed the door aside just enough so that my head was slightly visible above the top of the box. As I tipped the cup toward my parched lips, some of the cool water spilled down my neck.

It felt so good.

I poured a little more of the precious water out and let it run onto my shoulders and chest. Wasteful, yes and probably very foolish, but I couldn't stop myself.

I stuffed the fruit into my mouth so quickly that I barely took the time to appreciate its glorious taste. I just wanted to fill my stomach, which growled loudly even while I was shoveling the food in.

The ongoing battle in my bowels, which had felt like only a minor skirmish earlier, now raged like a war of epic proportions. From time to time, I farted out small amounts of foul intestinal gas, hoping to alleviate some of the pressure in my gut. Each time I did so, I worried that I might accidently shit and the last thing I needed was to flood my coffin with excrement. As it was, the stench coming out of me almost did me in.

My innards and I continued fighting throughout the long afternoon. My shit wanted to come out and say hello to the world. I refused to let it do so. Something had to give.

When full darkness finally settled around the boat, I decided I could wait no longer. I had to take care of business. With my ass cheeks clenched tightly and tears of joy streaming down my face, I tippy-toed to the edge of the roof and stuck my ass out as far over the edge as I possibly could and let loose.

Out spewed what can only be described politely as a monsoon of filth. Thank God I had chosen to go off the end of the ship that had walls beneath the roof. When I was finished, I had to let myself drip dry since I had nothing with which to wipe my ass.

Back in my rat-hole, feeling the weight of the world off of my shoulders and out of my intestines, I lay down and pulled the door shut across me. I could now comfortably wait a few more hours before I had to emerge from my hellhole once again.

My routine was now set. For the next two days I didn't diverge from it for any reason.

Around dusk on the third day, the sounds of boat traffic and people along the river began to steadily increase. Eventually these sounds became almost non-stop. I assumed that this meant we were entering the village of

Kapit. A few hours later that evening, the horn of the *Roi des Belges* let out three long bursts, signaling that we had indeed arrived in Kapit.

Shortly after the steamer docked, I heard Japanese voices emanating from below. I had picked up a little Japanese a few years earlier from my friend, Hoshi, a neighborhood kid, until he and his family were sent to the Manzanar internment camp in 1942. My interest in learning the language returned when I was stationed in Australia. I studied Japanese for about an hour or so every night before lights out. Although I knew a lot of the basics, I still wasn't very fluent. Now I tried to figure out what was being said below me.

Unfortunately I couldn't really understand Japanese when it was spoken rapidly. The only words my meager language skills allowed me to interpret were the words 'plane' and 'white.'

When the Japs mentioned Kantu's village, I assumed they were inquiring about me and my whereabouts. I heard what I thought was Kela's voice and then nothing but silence. I figured the Japs had left but wasn't sure. I forced myself to count slowly to one thousand.

Before I got to the end, Kela, Kantu and Batang secreted me off the boat and back into the jungle.

After walking for a while, we stopped.

"I can go no farther, men," Kela said a few miles outside of Kapit. "I must return to the steamboat in time for the morning trip back to Sibu."

I stuck my hand out. "Of course. We understand. You've already done so much for us. I just want to let you know how grateful I am for your assistance and the risk you took to get me safely to Kapit."

"It was the least I could do." He shook my hand.

"Goodbye, Kela," I said. "You've been very kind. I promise that we will meet again when the war is over."

Kela shrugged and lifted up his arms turning his palms upward. "Who knows what the future holds? I hope to see you again after all this horror has passed. Maybe then we can ask ourselves if these things really happened or if it was all just a terrible dream."

I stared deep into the eyes of this profound little man. "We few, we happy few, we band of brothers; for he today that sheds his blood with me shall be my brother, and you Kela are indeed my brother."

His crooked grin made him look sly and very, very pleased. "Henry the Fifth, it was my dad's favorite." Kela turned and walked away.

Chapter Twelve

Kantu, Batang, and I headed east, toward the interior highlands of Borneo, as we quick-stepped it along the jungle path, away from Kapit. Our plan was to travel all night under the cover of darkness. When the sun came up we would find a place to hide for the daylight hours. Once safely out of sight, we would eat, drink and rest until nightfall and then we would start out all over again. And that is exactly what we did for several days as we steadily moved into the highlands and into the unknown.

After a week of traveling only at night, we figured that we were far enough removed from the Japanese patrols around Kapit to start traveling by day instead of night. Trekking through the jungles of Borneo at night was not a wise proposition, but it was something that necessity had forced us to do. It was a good feeling to now know that whatever the jungle was about to throw at us at least we'd be able to see it coming and react accordingly. However, what lay immediately ahead of us we never saw coming because that's exactly how the Z-force intended for it to be.

Toward the end of our first full day of traveling in the light, we entered into an extremely heavy thicket of overgrown jungle. A dense wall of green leaves and beige vines hanging endlessly from the canopied jungle ceiling spread out in front of us. Kantu was at the front of our three man column. Because there was no real path, Kantu and Batang swung their machetes wildly back and forth like windshield wipers pushing aside the rain.

I tried to help as well, clearing the quagmire of greenery with my small sword. Sweat ran into my eyes and before long my shoulders ached. As I was about to call for a rest, the entire jungle in front of us seemed to shift and then a second later it stopped moving.

Machete raised in mid-swing, Kantu immediately stopped chopping and shifted his machete into a defensive position. Once again, the jungle seemed to shift, albeit ever so slightly. By then however, the moving jungle wasn't just in front of us anymore; it was now all around us.

Kantu, Batang and I formed a small circle with our backs pressed together. Each of us raised our weapons and waited to meet our fate.

Silence reigned for a full minute. My arm ached from holding the raised sword and I had so much sweat rolling in my eyes that I wasn't sure I could connect with anything even if it jumped out an inch before me.

"Put your weapons down," a man with an Australian accent shouted. A split second later, a tall, white man in Dayak attire accompanied by dozens of Borneo headhunters camouflaged perfectly to match the jungle environs, emerged all around us.

"Are you Z-force?" I asked the white man.

"Fair dinkum mate, Bunny Hobson, the magnificent, at your service." The Z-force commando and his allies shouldered their weapons as they came closer.

Kantu and Batang looked at each other, huge smiles of relief plastered on their faces. They had successfully delivered their precious allied cargo to the legendary Z-force.

"Mission accomplished, Flyer. Now we go home," Kantu said to me.

A confused look crossed Bunny's face. "What do they call you, mate?"

"Flyer," I said.

Bunny smiled. "Okay then, Flyer it is. But what's your given name?"

"Alexander Anderson," I replied

"You're a sight for sore eyes," I said as I rushed forward to shake Bunny's hand.

"I suspect I am, mate. You're looking a bit rough there. Had a tough time getting here?"

"Piece of cake," I grinned. "Speaking of cake, my friends and I are starved. We could do with a bit of grub if you have it to give."

"Pleasure's all mine, mate." Bunny ushered Kantu, Batang, and me away for a well-deserved rest and one of the best meals I'd had in weeks.

Chapter Thirteen

George Randolph Hobson, aka 'Bunny,' hailed from Queenscliff, a small coastal town near Manly Beach Australia. Because Bunny had some previous military training in the Australian Home Guard, he'd been recruited into the war effort by a top secret Allied organization called IASD in early 1943. He'd received commando training at a school near his home, called Camp Z. This secret training school was located in the Refuge Bay area just north of Sydney.

Z-force Special Unit, an offshoot of IASD—Inter-Allied Services Department—had been created specifically to conduct surveillance and sabotage activities in Borneo. Bunny had parachuted into the Borneo highlands in April

1945, shortly after his commander, Major Tom Harrisson, established a forward operating base.

The dozen or so commandos under Major Harrisson's command had split in order to cover more ground. Each commando was responsible for what went on in his own specific territory, and Bunny's area included the highlands near Mount Bawoei.

"We've been tracking you blokes for quite some time," Bunny said. "We almost had to introduce ourselves about three days back." He chuckled.

"What do you mean?" I asked.

"A Jap patrol less than a mile to your east was heading directly toward you fellas. My right hand man, Unka," he said as he nodded to the warrior next to him, "suggested we could probably redirect the Jap patrol by asking some of the local girls to bathe topless in the river and to make sure they did it loudly, with as many giggles and jiggles as they could muster to catch the attention of the horny little Jap bastards."

"And just like clockwork, when those tiny-dicked, slant-eyed fuckers heard women, they stopped their westward advance and made a beeline straight for the gals. I can't say I much blamed 'em, being out here in the middle of nowhere, with only a few native women around." Bunny sniggered. "Hell I've even got to admit that when I saw some of those pretty young Sheila's down by the river, with their wet titties jiggling about, I couldn't help but to pop a little fattie myself, if you know what I mean?"

Kantu, Batang and I nodded, each of us grinning. I could already tell that I was going to like this guy a lot. This tall man with piercing green eyes and a head full of slicked back hair could really tell a tale. He made everyone feel comfortable and more importantly-safe.

"Thanks," I said, "for both saving us and for the entertaining story."

"Don't thank me, thank Unka," Bunny said.

I looked over Bunny's left shoulder at Unka sitting on the ground behind him. He returned my gaze and nodded, then began struggling to pull something out of his burlap sack.

Bunny stood up and moved away from his aide de camp. "Unka's got a surprise for you."

Unka plucked a recently severed Japanese head out of the bag, like a magician pulling a rabbit out of a hat.

He laughed, sounding like a pig squealing for food.

My stomach lurched and I slapped my palm over my mouth.

The head was covered in a brownish bloody red slime. The Jap's eyes were partially opened and his mouth was forever frozen in a terrifying death grimace. Black flies swarmed around the stump of the neck.

Bunny apparently noticed my shock. He patted my arm. "Don't worry Flyer, it'll look and smell a lot better when he boils and shrinks it up. Won't have a damned fly anywhere on it by then. You'll see."

"Can't wait," I said, hating the insecurity in my voice. I struggled to recreate a normal look on my face.

Without warning, Unka pulled a slightly curved knife out of his waistband. He plunged it into the severed head. And then he did it again. And again, each stroke faster than the last. Chunks of flesh flew from the face, splattering in a growing, gruesome pile near his feet.

Smiling, Unka let loose a native mantra that made the hairs on my arms stand at attention.

"Slits, slits, slits, slits."

"Why is he doing that?" "What's he saying?" I asked Bunny, all pretense of comfort gone once again.

"Unka calls all Japs 'slits' because their eyes are shaped like tiny little slits carved into a normal human head. Unka's hatred of the Japs is a real set of dog's balls."

"A what?" I concentrated on Bunny's face now, trying to avoid the utter destruction that Unka was raining down upon the Jap's severed head.

"You know, mate, dog's balls—easy for everyone to see."

After his laughter died down, Bunny fished a photo out of his top pocket. "I keep it here because it's closest to my heart. Look here, mate, this is what I'm fighting for."

The photo showed Bunny laying on a beach with a beautiful woman by his side. A cigarette dangled between his lips as he stared out over the ocean.

"She's lovely," I said, somewhat taken aback to be staring at a photograph of a younger Bunny and a scantily clad gal while we were fighting Japs in the middle of the jungle.

"She's my wife." Bunny whispered in a soft voice as he carefully put the photo back into his shirt pocket.

"I'm just trying to get back to that. To that beach, to that girl, to that moment in time."

Weren't we all?

"What now?" I asked.

"Back to our jungle fortress. I'm tired and I bet you fellas are too."

Indeed I was.

Chapter Fourteen

Wasting virtually no time, Bunny marched our group eastward, deep into the highlands. The terrain was getting much steeper and the jungle more dense, which made our journey even more difficult. Throughout the ten mile hike that Bunny insisted we would make before nightfall, we constantly encountered Dayak pickets at their designated jungle checkpoints. Dayak and Borneo headhunters allied with the Z-force seemed to be everywhere.

Around sunset we arrived at Bunny's heavily guarded Z-force jungle compound.

It was incredibly mysterious to say the least. Women, children, and small animals filled the place. Goats and pigs wandered about freely and a huge water buffalo was tethered to a rubber tree next to a small stream. Two well hidden longhouses occupied each side of the stream. Bamboo sticks wrapped with dried leaves and cloth soaked in kerosene provided just enough light to see.

Nearly all the Dayak men were lean and fit and most were covered in tattoos from head to toe. The women paraded about topless, most with small children clinging to the breasts.

"You must visit my home." Bunny motioned for Kantu, Batang and me to follow him into a small cave. Two powerful Borneo headhunters guarded the entrance.

Unka nodded to them then led our small group into the cave.

Worn out, I dropped to the ground. Sitting on the woven mat felt amazing after the long, hard walk. Everyone else stretched out in front of a small fire in the center of the cave. Obviously not for warmth in the sweltering jungle, the fire instead was the cave's lone source of light. I attempted to stretch my legs out, like my brethren but precious little room remained. Arrayed around the fire as we were, our group cast eerie shadow images on the beige rock walls. Some of the shadows seemed to move in illogical and unexplainable directions.

I was probably just imaging it. Exhaustion had a way of doing that to me, and I can honestly say that I'd never felt as wiped out. And man was I ever hungry again.

Two old women entered bearing bowls of food. My stomach growled in happy anticipation.

Hopefully, supper wouldn't consist of vile Sago worms.

It didn't.

The women set a platter of what looked to be meat on a stick in front of us. They doled out *tuak*, as well. Dinner was shaping up to be excellent. I actually began to drool like a lion ready to tear into a wounded gazelle on the Serengeti.

Glancing at me, Bunny picked up one of the meat-covered sticks and took a bite. "Bog in, mate."

And bog in—whatever the hell that meant—I did. I tore into the fire blackened meat with reckless abandon. It was extremely delicious or maybe not. I didn't really know or care. I was a starving animal that needed to eat.

"Is this water buffalo?" I asked Bunny a little later, after I'd eaten nearly all the meat in front of me.

He smiled. "Wee bit smaller than that, mate."

"Okay," I said and furrowed my brow.

After a moment, Bunny chuckled. "It's rat."

"It's what?" Who knew rat could taste so good?

Afterward, we laid back and prepared to sleep. Bunny let the fire burn down and the cave fell into nearly complete darkness.

About the time I started to doze off, a noxious odor wafted over me. I turned my head from side to side, trying to figure out what it was and where it was coming from. And then I heard it.

Loud, wet-sounding farts gurgled from Unka's location. They continued in quick repetition, one after the other, for what seemed like a full minute. The stench was beyond horrific. I was fearful that the cave might explode from the combination of intestinal gas and fire embers.

No one seemed to be bothered by any of this except for me. Surely Unka had to know what he was doing, how it was affecting all of us even if no one said anything about it. Yet he just kept squirting out the stench without so much as a 'pardon me.'

Just as I was about to go sleep outside the cave, Bunny raised up on his elbows. "Unka, is that you, opening your lunch over there, mate?"

"Yes it truly is," Unka said as he farted again.

Bunny chuckled. "I know the Dayak believe that if you're hungry you eat, if you're tired you sleep, if you're randy you fuck, and if you need to fart you fart. But my nose and ears are just about done for. Out you go fella," Bunny said with humorous insistence.

"Oh, thank God," I said. I thought I would choke to death."

Everyone laughed and uttered similar sentiments.

Seeing that the rest of the group agreed wholeheartedly with Bunny's command decision, Unka sheepishly exited the cave.

After the air cleared, I slept the sleep of the dead.

I awoke feeling refreshed and invigorated by the hospitable surroundings. When I came out of the cave, Bunny was eating some fruit, and he encouraged me to join him for breakfast. I grabbed a banana and mango then sat by Bunny as he gazed into the moving water of the stream.

"So what's the plan?" I asked.

Bunny picked up a small piece of bamboo and drew a map in the dirt. "This is roughly where we are." He pointed to a spot on the crudely drawn map. "This is where we need to go." He slowly dragged the stick through the dirt, creating a line, from where we were to a place he called Mount Baowei.

"Harrisson is here." He indicated the spot with an X. "The major is constructing an airfield made out of bamboo, on top of the mountain. We'll eventually be able to bring in supplies and take out downed flyers like you. Problem is, it won't be completed for at least six more weeks."

I sighed. "What do we do until then?"

"We hang tight. We'll continue to reconnoiter this area for Japs, and maybe in a couple of days, we'll head back toward Kapit and blow up some shit. Until then, just relax and get your strength back, okay, mate?"

I nodded, though traveling back towards Kapit was the last thing I wanted to do.

I returned to the cave and found Kantu and Batang preparing to leave. Bunny's people had loaded them down with ample supplies that they now were trying to squeeze into their packs.

I couldn't take my eyes off of Kantu and Batang. Sadness about their imminent departure overwhelmed me. What could I possibly say to the men who'd saved my life numerous times? How could I ever repay them for the sacrifices they'd made and the chances they'd taken?

Nothing I could say or do would ever be enough. Of that I was certain.

And then I got an idea.

Perhaps I could give them something that would symbolize my gratefulness.

"Stay one more day, please," I said to Kantu and Batang.

Without hesitation, they nodded. Apparently, they were also upset about our parting.

"Wait, here. I need to talk to Bunny and then I'll be right back."

After Bunny gave me all the necessary information, I returned to my friends.

"I'll meet you in front of the longhouses in an hour."

"What you planning, Flyer?" Kantu asked, eyes glittering with apparent anticipation.

"It's a secret."

I took off running.

Chapter Fifteen

I found the local shaman, right where Bunny said I would. I explained my plan and asked if he could help. He agreed and said he would meet me, along with two of his assistants, at the appointed hour.

At the longhouse, my friends jumped up and greeted me when I returned. Manang and two young acolytes rounded the corner and joined us.

"Kantu, Batang, my two most cherished friends. We're going to get matching tattoos!" Realizing the importance of tattoos to the Dayak, I explained to my brothers that I wanted the three of us to each get the same tattoo to symbolize our friendship. I told them that this would be sort of an ink bond of unity that would link us together forever.

Kantu and Batang looked at each other and then nodded enthusiastically. "Is good idea, Flyer," Batang said.

With a stick, I sketched the Chi Rho symbol in the dirt. "The Chi Rho is one of the oldest Christograms known to man. Emperor Constantine dreamed about this divine symbol just before the famous Battle of Milvian Bridge in 312 AD. He had his soldiers paint the Chi Rho on their shields for protection. It worked and he was victorious in battle. Constantine was sure that God had protected his own because of this symbol."

"This Chi Rho will protect us from Japs?" Kantu asked.

"That is my hope. But I want to add something else to it." I dragged my stick through the ground again until I was satisfied with the drawing.

Batang furrowed his brow. "What is this?"

"A few years ago I saw a coin in a museum emblazoned with the Chi Rho symbol and the Alpha and

Omega symbols on each side of it. When Jesus proclaimed that he was the son of God he did so by saying that he was the Alpha and Omega, the beginning and the end. I want to add the alpha and omega symbols so that we will always be reminded of how we began and how we ended."

They smiled and, a moment later, enfolded me in a very unexpected but welcomed embrace.

Who said you couldn't teach old dogs some new tricks?

Chapter Sixteen

We watched the Shaman prepare the ink for our tattoos. The Dayak used various ingredients to make their dark ink. Mostly they used the ash of Ku Kui nuts and mixed it with coconut oil. Sometime they used soot from burned candles mixed with charcoal and honey from bee hives. Our shaman used a combination of all the above.

The tattoos would be hand tapped into the underside of our right forearms with the aid of two bamboo sticks. One stick was thin and delicate with sharpened needlelike ridges cut out of it. The other was more substantial and served as a hammering instrument. The Shaman estimated that the painful tattooing process would take anywhere from four to six hours to complete.

The acolyte artists helping offered us an inordinate amount of *tuak* before the actual tattooing began.

"Drink up, boys," Bunny said, tipping back his own cup. "This is Borneo's finest chloroform."

He didn't have to tell us twice. We drained our cups only to find them refilled an instant later.

The Shaman instructed us to lay flat on our backs. As I settled myself on a brightly colored woven man, a group of women entered the longhouse and began playing an assortment of *sapes*, gongs, and cymbals. Potent incense burned in holders all around us.

It was decided that the Shaman would do my tattoo and each of the acolytes would work on one of my brothers. I closed my eyes and felt myself sinking into the mat, covered with delicious smells and sounds.

Such bliss. And then the Shaman began digging into my arm with the bamboo awl and bliss quickly turned into hell.

Tears welled in my eyes. "Would you stop for just a moment," I said through clenched teeth.

He just looked at me and smiled, then continued on for what felt like an eternity.

I looked over to see how Kantu and Batang were handling this black-inked torture.

What the hell?

They were sound asleep. Tough guys.

I had to be the world's biggest pussy. All I wanted to do was yank my arm back and scream like a little girl. What had possessed me to have a tattoo scratched into my arm with a bamboo needle? And why had I created such a damned big design?

The Shaman must have taken pity on me then. He waved to one of the women holding the *tuak*. "He need."

Oh, yes I did. I chugged it down.

"He need more," he said when I flinched again.

I guzzled three more cupfuls then stretched back out and tried to ignore the burning in my arm.

Four and a half hours later, the tatoos were finished.

Kantu, Batang and I were now inextricably linked together forever.

The pustules of blood bubbling up from our brand new tattoos began to dry. Once the bleeding had stopped, the Dayak helpers rubbed aloe on our punctures to help the healing process along. Our arms were bandaged with cotton held in place with a small piece of string.

That night Kantu, Batang and I sat around a small fire, drinking more *tuak* and talking about life. We promised each other that after the war we'd see each other again, somehow, someway.

Eventually we settled to sleep on a soft bed of flat rubber tree leaves, just outside of Bunny's cave. The sky was as majestic as the face of God, and the canopy of ultra-bright twinkling stars were as pure as tears poking holes in the blackness overhead. As always, the Big Dipper seemed to shine the brightest. I knew I was feeling overly sentimental, probably the result of the incredible amount of *tuak* I'd drunk over the past few hours. As the sky above began to spin round and round, I closed my eyes and went to sleep.

When I awoke at sunrise, Kantu and Batang were gone.

I was angry and confused that they hadn't bothered to say goodbye to me in some grand and melodramatic fashion. My anger however, diminished throughout the course of the day, along with my hangover. I had to remember, Batang and Kantu were from a distinctly different culture than my own. Their way wasn't my way. And that was okay. And even if it wasn't, I needed to get over it.

Chapter Seventeen

I moped around for the next few days, feeling sorry for myself. I missed the company of my brothers and wasn't about to apologize for it.

Apparently sensing my loneliness, Bunny seemed to be making a point of spending a lot of time with me. We ate all our meals together and talked in depth about the war, my plane crash, and, of course, about his beloved family back in Oz.

Bunny was twenty six years old, only seven years older than I was. Married since he was twenty, he already had two young sons, Noah and Thorpe. He seemed to miss them much like I missed Kantu and Batang. And his love for his wife was something he never tired of expressing. He showed me the photo of the two of them on the beach once again, holding it carefully as one would cradle a newborn.

I treasured the time I now spent with Bunny. He was funny, dashing and handsome. He made everyone feel safe as if he was always in control. I loved the Australian slang he used to describe virtually everything. I called them 'Bunnyisms.' He had quickly become my new best friend, and it wasn't long before my grief over the departure of my brothers Kantu and Batang began to wane.

About a week after Kantu and Batang had left, Bunny asked if I wanted to go out with his 'crew,' as he called them, and help reconnoiter a Jap radio transmitting station up in the mountains.

"Hell yes!" I said, infusing more enthusiasm in my voice that I really felt. It was great that Bunny saw me as an equal and that he wanted me to be part of his team. But I knew I wasn't really in the same league as him. Nevertheless, I agreed to accompany Bunny and the others on their mission. The crew would consist of Me, Bunny, Unka and two headhunters. The headhunters would be equipped with only their machetes and blowpipes.

Before we left, Bunny pulled me into his cave. "You ever use one of these, mate?" He handed me a machine gun.

I slowly ran my left hand over the cool metal of the weapon. "Nope"

"This here is called the Diggers Darling," he said. "It's an Owen 9-mm submachine gun."

"It's heavy," I said, hefting it against my shoulder before handing it back to him.

He nodded. "Nine and a half pounds, to be exact. This magazine on top," he pointed, "holds thirty two rounds. It's the most reliable gun in the whole damn shooting match. Before they issued them to me and the boys, they dragged 'em through mud and sand to make sure they worked even in the absolute worst jungle conditions."

He showed me how to put the magazine on and take it off. He showed me where the safety was located.

"When you fire it, hold it close to your chest and stomach. Firmly squeeze the trigger and don't let up until you mow down every bloody Nip in front of you."

I felt the blood drain out of my face. In all this time I still hadn't had to kill anyone face to face.

"Aw, no worries, mate," he said, apparently seeing the trepidation on my face. "She'll be apples. You'll see."

I guess he was trying to tell me everything would be just fine. But how could he know for sure?

We'd take out the desolate Jap transmitting station in the mountains if it was lightly guarded. However, if it was heavily fortified, we were to map its coordinates and wait for reinforcements before launching our assault. These orders came directly from Major Harrisson.

Dayak reconnaissance suggested that as few as five or six Japs were guarding the radio tower. "It shouldn't be too hard for the five of us to whip their yellow asses," Bunny said. He figured the whole deal would take about one week to complete—two days to get there, a day to take out the tower and then two more days to return back to camp.

"We still have at least five weeks to kill until the airstrip is finished. I might as well kill some Japs, while I'm here," I said, feigned bravado coloring my words.

Could I do it? Only time and circumstances would tell.

"That's the spirit, mate." Bunny clapped me on the back and seemed not to notice my nervousness. Or maybe he did. But he was savvy enough not to mention it.

Before we set off, Bunny removed the picture of his wife from his pocket and took off his wedding band. He set them on top of his bed pallet. "You too, Flyer," he said nodding in my direction. "Ditch the ring and anything else you might have on you that could identify you. If the mission goes south, we don't want the Japs knowing who we are."

"Okay," I said, reluctantly removing my high school ring. It was the only thing I had left from my old life and letting it go now, even if only temporarily, felt strange. All my memories of Freddy and Betty and everyone else back home were part of that ring.

"Where should I put it?"

"Drop it on top of my photograph, next to my ring. It'll be safe here, I promise."

I sighed and did as I was told. High school felt like another world, a world that no loner existed. Betty's tit's now seemed light years away. But what I wouldn't give to be back in my crappy little hometown right about now.

Chapter Eighteen

The first day of the march was brutally hot and humid. I mean it was jungle hot and jungle humid. I'd been sweating like a pig since sunrise. By noon, my lips felt cracked and I was lightheaded and shaky. I needed water.

"I have to stop, Bunny. I gotta rest." I didn't want to tell him that I'd finished my water an hour earlier. He was always telling me to pace myself. Dammit, he'd been right.

Bunny looked at me then signaled to one of the headhunters. "Scout the immediate area in front of us for the yellow dog."

I plopped down on the ground.

Bunny remained upright, poised to spring into battle should the need arise.

The scout soon returned, flashing a thumbs up.

Bunny nodded, seemingly to himself. "Okay, five minutes." He pushed his chin out and looked at me again. "Time to liquefy, Flyer. My throat is as dry as a bloody dead dingo's donger."

Most of the time I didn't know what in the hell Bunny was saying when he spoke his crazy Australian slang, but this time I knew exactly what he meant even if I didn't understand any of the words.

After he took a long pull from his water canteen, he handed it to me. "I told you to pace yourself." He sounded not as much like he was scolding me now but more like he was concerned about my health.

I drank a little water then held the canteen out to him.

"Go on, mate. Have a bit more. You look as parched as my granny's twat."

How he knew what his granny's twat looked like, I didn't want to know, and I tried to push the image out of my head while taking a final, grateful swallow of the best tasting water I'd ever had.

Before I knew it, our break was over. Bunny had us up and on the march again. By nightfall, after we'd found a spring of cool water and I'd refilled my canteen to the brim, we were within a few kilometers of the radio station. We set up camp for the night. No fire would be built and everyone would have to take a turn at watch.

Bunny and I found a small clearing and bedded down under low hanging branches.

Unka took the first three-hour watch, scurrying up a large palm tree in a matter of seconds, as if it were only a slight incline. I watched him as he made a cozy little crow's nest among the branches. It looked like he was high enough to see almost everything around us and the floppy green leaves concealed his position nicely.

The two headhunters simply melted into the jungle, their whereabouts unknown. They never stayed in camp nor did they ever say where they would be, yet they always seemed to be around whenever we needed them.

As the jungle sky darkened and the heavenly lights above assumed their proper places on stage, Bunny and I found ourselves quietly whispering to each other, in deep conversation. Mostly Bunny spoke while I listened. His usual upbeat optimism now seemed suddenly tainted with hopelessness and despair. He peppered his rambling comments about his wife and kids with more melancholy than I'd ever heard from him.

It was downright creepy, and I wished he would stop.

Bunny rubbed the area where his wedding band usually was. This went on for quite some time before he finally stopped fidgeting. By then he'd turned his eyes toward the heavens above and just stared as if the answers to every question never asked were up there.

"It's pretty," he said, startling me with his first words in nearly ten minutes.

"What?"

"The full moon, mate." He pointed then went silent again, just staring. "You know, Flyer," he said after a moment, "it's kind of crazy if you think about it. My wife and boys are so terribly beyond the black stump it's hard to even imagine their whereabouts. Yet, at this very moment, when they look up and gaze into the night sky, they see the very same moon that I'm looking at right now. That's bloody amazing, don't you think?"

"I guess so."

"I'd give just about anything for a quick pash and shag with the wifey right about now." He sounded wistful.

"Why the fuck are you talking this way?"

"Let's get real, Flyer. Who are we kidding? You and I are totally rooted out here in this God forsaken jungle. The chances of either of us surviving the war are basically slim to none. This war's going to go on forever and a day, and if the Japs don't get us, bloody disease eventually will."

I shook my head. "You're wrong. We've beaten the Japs back across the Pacific, and soon we'll take the fight directly to their home islands. MacArthur had already recaptured the P.I., and the Nazis are pretty much done for. Your family is safe and sound back in Oz, and they're waiting for you to come home. You can't give up now. All we have to do is ride out the remainder of this shit fracas and we'll be fine. And when we take out those Jap fuckers tomorrow, we'll be one step closer to home."

Bunny chuffed out a sound that I couldn't decipher. He was either scoffing at my words or mulling them over in apparent agreement. "Maybe you're right, Flyer. Maybe you're right. Okay then, enough of this ear bashing, let's

stop yabberin' on and get some sleep."

I did not sleep that night.

Chapter Nineteen

The five of us set out a few hours before sunrise. Bunny wanted the assault to begin right before dawn. Our crew operated best under the cover of darkness.

After an hour's walk through the jungle, the headhunter on point informed Bunny that we had arrived at the attack site. He led us up a small embankment then pulled aside some large elephant ear leaves in front of us and pointed. The Jap tower appeared directly before us.

Unka looked at Bunny and smiled that curious sadistic smile of his while he dragged his index finger across his throat in a slicing motion. His excitement about the prospect of killing some Jap was obvious.

Bunny's plan of attack was simple and straightforward. Unka would climb up the radio tower and quietly dispatch its lone sentry. With any luck the guard might even be asleep. Unka would stay atop the tower and watch for approaching Jap reinforcements. The headhunters would be sent forward, to the single room radio station, where the rest of the Japs slept.

Bunny handed each of us what the Aussies called a Mill's Bomb hand grenade. These pineapple shaped explosives packed a real wallop. The headhunters were to toss their grenades through the barrack's windows. They would then have about four seconds to take cover. Because the attack was occurring just before dawn, Bunny believed that all the Japs would be sleeping and that there would be almost no chance for a possible grenade throwback, which unfortunately happened from time to time.

Bunny would cover the back exit of the building with his 9-mm Owen sub machine gun. I was to stay in the jungle, out of harm's way, and observe the operation from afar.

Sounded good to me, especially the part about staying out of harm's way.

Bunny looked down at my gun. "You do remember how to use that, right?"

"Yeah, sure, of course." Good Lord willing, I wouldn't have to.

"Do not move from here or get involved unless it is absolutely essential," Bunny said.

I shook my head. "You got it, boss." That wasn't going to be a problem. I planned to glue myself to this spot.

After everyone checked their equipment one last time, Unka and the others headed out to start the party.

The attack began seconds later, thirty minutes before sunrise.

Unka darted from tree to tree, across the compound, until he finally arrived at the base of the radio tower. He didn't use the steps leading up to the guard platform up top. Instead, he climbed along the outside part of the wooden scaffolding. Once he got to the platform, he pulled himself up alongside the outer wall and peeked over the edge into the tower.

He signaled to Bunny, who was poised to break from the jungle and make for the back of the radio building, that the tower was empty.

Even from fifty feet away, I could see the tension increasing in Bunny's posture.

At that instant, the door to the outhouse below the tower opened. The Jap sentry, still fixing his drawers, popped out. He'd been in there, shitting or doing something else, for as long as the crew and I had been here—at least the last half hour.

Unka noticed the guard about the same time that Bunny and I did. As the guard started up the steps, Unka climbed over the small wall and onto the platform. He ducked down and disappeared from sight.

When the sentry reached the top platform, faint sounds of a struggle reached me, but they only lasted less than half a minute. Then silence dropped over everything like a shroud.

Two minutes later, a Jap head flew from the tower and landed with a thud near the outhouse. Unka stood up then and smiled broadly. He waved his bloody machete back and forth and started doing a silly little dance he called the *Dead-Jap-Jig*.

Bunny motioned for the headhunters to move forward. They sprinted across the compound and positioned themselves underneath the windows of the radio building. Bunny also ran toward the building. I couldn't see him now but assumed he was getting into position to cover any attempt at escape from the rear of the building.

The headhunters nodded to each other, pulled the pins on their grenades, and lobbed them into the building.

As they threw themselves to the ground, a terrific explosion sounded and the air filled with the stench of smoke and fire.

As quickly as it had begun, the mission was over.

I rejoined my comrades just as Bunny kicked in the back door and sprayed the inside of the room with a volley of bullets from his Owen sub machine gun.

"I told you to stay put," he growled when I appeared by his side.

"But you did it," I said, my enthusiasm bubbling like that of a child at his own birthday party. "The mission is over, and I'm still safe and sound."

He grumbled and shook his head. "We're not done yet, jackass." Bunny shoved me backward then turned away from me. Crouched, he slowly entered the cloudy, smoke filled ruins.

I waited outside.

Seconds later, another short burst of gunfire ensued.

I could see Bunny standing in the middle of the smoky room.

"Now we're done," Bunny called to me as my ears still echoed from the nearby machine gun blasts. "Get your ass in here, mate."

I ran into the room.

Bunny systematically destroyed the radio and its components, while he ordered me and the crew to gather up every single piece of paper we could find. Less than five minutes later, we had pocketed everything possible and moved out of the smoldering building, the inside of which smelled like burnt meat.

As we were exiting the compound, Unka grabbed the Jap head he'd severed and stuffed it into his sacred black sack. He looked at me and dragged his index finger across his throat. "Slits all dead," he said, grinning.

We then ran for a full ten minutes, putting as much distance between us and the compound as we possibly could.

"Figjam, that's what I am," Bunny said, after we'd stopped to rest and gather ourselves.

"What?" I asked.

"Figjam," he said again slowly and with emphasis, like a drunk trying to appear sober.

"What's figjam?" I asked again.

"Fuck, I'm great, just ask me," he bellowed and then let loose a loud guffaw.

The headhunters smiled from ear to ear.

Unka stroked the severed head through its sack and looked as if he were in the midst of ecstasy.

And I felt, well, I didn't know what I felt. For the first time during the entire war, I'd seen what savagery on the ground was really like. Prior to today, I had only been a casual participant of the war, flying safely above it. Now, I was knee deep in shit and not sure I liked the smell of it.

I stared at Bunny and the others, each still reveling in our recent success. I was sure I wasn't feeling the same level of exhilaration as them. And, truth be told, I never wanted to.

One thing was for certain; today's sights, smells, and sounds would haunt me forever no matter how hard I tried to forget them.

Chapter Twenty

The all too familiar, high pitched sound of the Japanese 50-mm, Type 96 light machine guns raked my ears, leaving them ringing. Bullets whizzed past me. Some even plucked at my shirt.

We had walked right into a Japanese ambush.

Out of the corner of my eye, in a moment of stunning clarity, during a time of utter chaos, I saw a hand appear from behind a tree. A second later it lobbed a grenade directly at us.

I hit the dirt and tried to make myself small and invisible.

And then the world, at least the one around me, exploded. Dirt flew everywhere.

An instant later I lifted up my head. To my right, Bunny was hunched over, on his knees, rubbing his ears. Blood spurted from his nose, covering his lips and chin in a sickening crimson display. As I struggled to my feet, my own blood trickled into my eyes and I couldn't hear a thing.

The Dayak headhunters had been killed instantly. One of them had been cut completely in half by the grenade. His mangled torso rested upright on the ground as if emerging from Hell itself, human entrails spilling out of his upper-body. Unka, badly injured by shrapnel to his chest and upper arms, had somehow managed to keep standing throughout the entire attack, though he seemed to be swaying and looked ready to fall at any second. Amazingly, he still clutched the black sack that contained his beloved war prize.

Bunny's intuition from the previous night had come to fruition. We were now prisoners of war.

The Japanese soldiers forced our arms down by our sides before securing a thick rope around our chests. Rifle butt punches rained down on us until we collapsed onto the ground. Bunny had been hit so hard in the jaw that a two of his teeth lay on the ground next to him. The rest had been smashed into bloody shards.

I curled myself into a ball on my side. My ribs were badly bruised. For a moment, nothing happened and I dared hope that they were finished beating us.

I was wrong.

The soldiers started kicking us and they didn't stop until the Jap in charge ordered them to stop.

The soldiers were instructed to roll us onto our backs and search us.

When they discovered the severed head in Unka's bag, the Jap leader let loose a litany of screaming, spittle flew from his lips. I had no idea what he was saying, but the meaning was clear as glass. He was furious and we were going to pay for our crimes.

The Jap in charge aimed his pistol at my face.

Knowing this was likely the end, I forced myself to maintain eye contact. I had nothing left to lose. At least I would know that I had died facing the enemy like a man.

"Who committed this atrocity," the man asked in heavily accented English.

I glared at him. "You did, when you attacked Pearl Harbor in '41."

With his gun still trained on me, he seemed to consider my words.

My heart skipped a beat. Had I just bought myself a bullet to the brain?

Without warning, he turned slightly and fired the pistol into the ground, next to Bunny's head.

"I won't miss next time," he said through clenched teeth. He adjusted the aim to the center of Bunny's chest.

I closed my eyes tightly as if that could block this horrific scene from unfolding.

"Me," Unka said. He began to laugh. "I kill slits."

Tears sneaked past my closed lids and tracked down my cheeks. I was certain that Unka would never see nightfall.

The Japs pulled Unka up and dragged him away from us but not so far that we couldn't see. Two guards held him up and a third kicked him behind the legs. Unka dropped to his knees then collapsed forward, falling face first into the dirt. One of the guards grabbed him by the hair and yanked him back up to a kneeling position. Unka began coughing up dirt and saliva, and bloody drool slowly dripped from his mouth.

The Jap in charge stood directly above Unka. He pulled his shin gunto sword out of its sheath and poured water from a canteen across the blade. He shouted something in Japanese.

With great pomp and precision, he raised the sword high above his head. At that instant Unka looked up and grinned. "Fuck you!" he yelled as the shin gunto blade began its downward arc. It sliced cleanly through his neck and, and in an instant, Unka was no more.

Chapter Twenty-One

After the assassination of Unka, I lay unconscious for nearly two days. Apparently the Japs carried me out of the jungle highlands on some rickety jerry-rigged stretcher, all the way back to Kapit. When I finally came to, I found myself lying on the floor of a longhouse staring out at the Rajang River.

My vision was pretty blurred and I ached from head to toe. I couldn't get up even if I'd wanted to. And I most surely didn't. I was surrounded by about a half dozen Jap guards. Bunny was nowhere in sight.

I couldn't remember ever being so thirsty. What word did the Japs use for water? I tried to summon it to mind. It began with an M, or at least I thought it did. I tried to remember every Jap word I knew that began with the letter M.

It finally came to me. 'Mizu.' Would the Japs give me water if I asked or should I just suffer in silence? It was a real Hobson's choice—either I could suffer from thirst or suffer from the beating the Japs might give me if I asked for water.

I looked at the three guards closest to me, trying to gauge which one might be the kindest, which one had the most amiable face and the gentlest disposition. I chose the youngest one.

I stared at him then, waiting for our eyes to meet. When they did, I nodded and forced a smile.

He stood up and approached me.

I tried to speak but no words came from my parched mouth. I mustered up what little bit of spit I could and swallowed. "Mizu," I said, barely whispering.

The young guard tilted his head and stared at me, perhaps bewildered that I had spoken to him in Japanese. He smiled and threw his head back, then cackled the most evil laugh I have ever heard.

"Mizu, Onegai shimasu mizu," I whispered again.

He held up his canteen as if to ask, is this what you want? He then looked at his buddies and chuckled, and soon everyone but me was laughing.

I nodded, cautiously hopeful that he might actually give me a drink.

He stood directly above me and twisted off the canteen's cap. When he saw in my eyes that I was convinced I was about to get a sip of water, he turned the canteen upside down and poured its contents onto the ground, just to the side of my face. He kicked me in the stomach with his steel-toed boot then slowly returned to his chair. My already fractured ribs throbbed and, in that moment, all I wanted to do was die.

"Mizu," he said, mocking me. He spit in my direction and laughed again.

I looked away, turning my head to the other side. After a while, I could hear that they had returned to their game of cards. When I thought no one was looking, I lapped up the tiny bit of water puddled on the ground next to me.

Later in the day, the Japs allowed an old Dayak woman to give me some water and a handful of rice. After I spilled a single grain of rice, I struggled to my knees so I could retrieve it. I put that grain of rice on the tip of my tongue and held it there for as long as I could before it eventually dissolved into a dot of tasteless paste. And with the ending of that meal my mind slipped away into a state of hallucinatory bliss.

I was back in high school, in Mr. West's comparative religion class.

My teacher was standing in front of a roomful of bored teenagers who seemed less than interested in what he had to say.

"Buddha survived for six years by eating only a single grain of rice and a sesame seed each day," he said.

Who cared about Buddha anyway?

Mr. West continued, "However even the Buddha eventually realized that this suffering was way too extreme and probably not the best path to true enlightenment. Perhaps there was a better way—a middle path to enlightenment. Buddha, of course, always had a choice regarding his ascetic behavior. It was self-imposed and of his own volition, whereas yours, Alex, is not."

The classroom door then opened and Betty Grable, clad in an overly tight sweater, entered and made her way toward my desk. She knelt beside me and ran her fingers through my hair. She stroked my cheek with her perfectly manicured index finger.

"Are you going to do it or not?" Freddy asked.

"You, have no such choice, Alex." Betty sighed minty breath into my face. "You are a prisoner of the Imperial Nation of Japan. If you wish to achieve enlightenment, you must stay alive, one grain of rice at a time. Stay alive, Alex, stay alive."

I looked up just in time to see Mr. West wink at me and smile then everything faded to black.

Chapter Twenty-Two

The next day the Japs dragged me from the longhouse and tossed me onto a flat-topped river barge. I was to be transported back down the Rajang River, to the village of Sibu.

The powerful diesel engines of the Jap barge sent gigantic plumes of noxious black smoke into the air. As the barge pulled away from the dock, I noticed another white man out of the corner of my eye.

Bunny.

He was still alive if just barely. His hair seemed to be matted with small knots of dried blood and dirt. Bruises covered most of his skin. His eyes were barely visible amidst the swollen folds of purple on either side of his nose.

Before I could get his attention, a Jap guard jostled me forward with the toe of his boot. Bunny raised his gaze in my direction and a moment later grinned, exposing his missing teeth.

"You here on holiday, mate?"

The Jap guard standing to Bunny's right slammed a thick, wooden baton into Bunny's stomach to silence him.

Bunny collapsed to his knees.

Two guards picked him up and stood him in front of one of two wooden poles that had been attached to the barge's bow. Using heavy rope, they lashed Bunny to one of the posts. His body leaned so far forward that he was almost dangling over the front edge of the vessel.

The Japs tightened the ropes, jerking Bunny back into a completely upright position.

They did the same thing to me on the other side of the bow. Firmly tethered to the eight foot poles, I'm sure we looked like some strange mastheads on the front of an old sailing ship.

"Lucky us, mate," Bunny said. "We're the trophies on display. It's the Japs way of trying to convince the indigenous folks that Japan is winning the war."

"Yeah, lucky us."

After enduring two days of this macabre display of Jap torture, Bunny and I were just about done. We had shit ourselves beneath the unrelenting tropical sun. Unpredictable periods of unconsciousness provided the briefest of respite from the nonstop agony.

A horn blasted nearby.

The trumpet of Gabriel? Was I about to go home to sweet Jesus? Please let it be so. I was more than ready.

I lifted up my head, happy to meet my maker.

All I saw was the steamer *Roi des Belges* heading directly toward us. Kela stood on the deck, less than fifteen feet away. He looked straight at me, horror etched into his face as the two ships closely passed one another. And then he and the *Roi des Belges* were gone.

I felt our barge slowing down several hours after we had passed the *Roi des Belges*. A group of Jap soldiers stood on a pier, about three hundred yards ahead. The barge docked and the soldiers climbed on board. One of them was a Colonel. The other Japs already onboard immediately snapped to attention.

"Bring me the person in charge of the prisoners!" The Colonel yelled, his tone harsh. He made his way over to Bunny and me and looked at us from head to toe.

By then the Jap Major in charge of our transportation appeared, shoulders slumped, eyes downcast in a deferential semi-bow. I couldn't understand much of the conversation, but they seemed to be talking about the decrepit state of Bunny and myself. My supposition seemed to be confirmed when the Jap Colonel struck the Major with a small bamboo riding crop he held in his right hand.

Between apologizes, the Major bowed over and over again.

Perhaps the Colonel realized that since the Japs were getting their asses handed to them all over the Pacific it was just a matter of time before the Allies gained control of Borneo. Maybe he thought that this public display of humanity would help him out during his inevitable war crimes trial. Or maybe he was just having a bad day. Who knew?

After the Colonel let loose a string of Jap jabber at the two petrified looking guards, they rushed over to Bunny and me and cut us away from the poles. We were helped by other guards to a shaded area at the rear of the barge. There, we were given fruit and fresh water and allowed to rest on small woven mats. We remained in the shaded area until the next day, when we reached Sibu.

Chapter Twenty-Three

Sibu was a much larger village than I remembered. I didn't see any of the headhunters who'd previously helped me. Strange, since they usually inundated this area. Had the Japs discovered my helpers and wiped them out? Or had the headhunters simply relocated to fight in another region? It wasn't likely that I'd get answers any time soon.

Bunny and I were taken to a well-guarded longhouse and slowly nursed back to decent health by a kindly Dayak woman. I ate as many Sago worms as I possibly could during this time. I knew that I needed every bit of the protein they provided, and I was now grateful for the creamy white larvae.

After a few days in isolation, Bunny and I were reunited in the common room during a meal. This was the first I'd seen of him in days and my heart quickened when he hobbled toward me.

"Holy Dooley, it's great to see you, Flyer. I thought you had carked for sure, but I'm sure glad to see that isn't so."

He obviously didn't remember asking me earlier if I was here on vacation.

I smiled at Bunny. "Nope, I'm still alive and kicking, a little banged up, but that's about it. You?"

"Other than the fact that my ears are ringing like crazy and a few of my teeth are missing, I feel like a bloody Mallee bull." He smiled broadly, revealing his missing teeth. "Gummed food tastes better, mate. Hangs around longer in my mouth, gives me more time to savor it." He snorted.

The old, wisecracking Bunny that I'd come to know and love was back. Thank God.

Bunny's face suddenly turned somber as he grabbed a handful of worms and rice. "Tell me what you remember?" He put the glob of the wormy-rice in his mouth. "Where are Unka and the other fellas?" he said as his gums mashed the food around in his mouth.

My skin began to crawl. Knowing how close he had been to Unka and the others, I just didn't know what to say. Maybe I should treat this like I would a nasty bandage that needed to be removed— just rip it off and get it over with. But could he handle it?

I took a deep breath. "They're all dead. The boys were killed instantly by a grenade. Unka was badly injured and barely alive after the attack. When the Japs found that severed head he was carrying around they put him down on his knees and beheaded him straight away."

Suprisingly, Bunny's face broke into a smile. He even chuckled a bit. "So how did the old boy go out?"

"Defiantly!" I sighed. "Yelling 'fuck you' at the top of his lungs."

Bunny threw back his head and looked toward the heavens. "Man, that crazy bloke was as mad as a cut snake and as mean as cat's piss. He really despised those filthy nips, didn't he?"

"Indeed, he did."

Bunny slowly turned his face away from me. "Well good on him," he mumbled. "I'm going to miss that magnificent brown bastard."

I put my hand on Bunny's shoulder. "Me too, me too."

Bunny brushed at his cheek with the back of his hand and stared at the floor and, for a moment, we were both silent, each of us grieving Unka in our own way.

"What now?" I asked after I noticed that Bunny was staring at me.

His shoulders slumped and he shook his head. "I don't know, Flyer." He suddenly sounded as dejected as I felt.

"Any chance Harrisson and his people will come looking for us?"

"Don't think so, mate."

"How can you be so sure?"

Bunny sighed. "Whenever the crew and I went on missions, I usually carried a cyanide capsule just in case I was captured. This was on orders from the boys up top. We were privy to so much classified shit that our being taken alive might jeopardize numerous operations throughout Borneo. Everyone in Z-force knew that if the Japs found out who we really were, the torture wouldn't stop until they got all the information they wanted. I lost the capsule during the ambush melee. Now look at me—a prisoner of war."

By now, my jaw had dropped open. "So they won't come because they expect that you're already dead."

"That's about right, mate. And when the nips find out who I really am, I will be dead for sure."

He wasn't the only one facing the same death sentence. I thought back to the arrival of the Colonel on the steamboat. I'd deluded myself then into thinking that he'd helped us because he knew that the war's end was near and that he might be trying to atone for a multitude of past sins. Now I was certain that the Jap Colonel had acted with more sinister intentions than his display of compassion had implied.

Shit.

I explained my theory to Bunny, who thankfully had no memories of our time tied to the posts on the boat. "I think the Japs know exactly who we are—that I am the downed aviator and that you are a Z-force commando. That's why they're taking such good care of us all of the sudden. They assume we've got valuable information. I know those sons of bitches are desperate for info about my plane's Norden bombsight, and you know they're dying to get specific intelligence about Z-force ops in the region."

"We're fucked," Bunny said.

Indeed, we were.

Chapter Twenty-Four

The next day Bunny and I were put onto a flatbed truck and driven through the hilly roads, to the small coastal village of Kabong, located on the South China Sea. The Jap guards dumped us at a small pier, in the middle of a harbor filled with all kinds of fishing boats.

Unceremoniously and without warning, the Japs pushed us into a steam-powered fishing boat that apparently had been hired out to serve as our transport. The vessel, which had been converted to diesel, spouted huge plumes of greasy, black smoke. A two story wheelhouse structure was located about a third of the way back. Directly behind that, running about twenty feet to the stern, was an outdoor space that the Japs had covered with a simple canvas awning. This was where Bunny and I were kept under constant guard. The Japs intended to take us across the large bay, to Kuching, and after that, presumably to the Batu Lintang Prisoner of War camp where we would no doubt be interrogated.

The first two days at sea passed uneventfully though both Bunny and I noticed that the farther out to sea we got, the more relaxed the guards seemed to become. It wasn't that they were friendly or even kind to us. However, by simply not being abusive, sadistic brutes with machine hearts and machine minds, they provided Bunny and me with a brief period of restful solace. They offered us food and water at regular intervals and occasionally even gave us candy and cigarettes.

After everything we'd already endured at the hands of the Japs this kind behavior seemed downright bizarre if not completely bizarre.

Every so often, one of the guards who spoke a little bit of English asked me questions about the United States.

He seemed especially curious about Hollywood and all its movie stars. For some asinine reason, he seemed to think that all Americans knew each other.

"Hey, Yankee you know Clark Gable?" he asked. "You ever make *fucky* with Myrna Loy?"

I nodded and laughed, hoping not to agitate him. Stupid Jap beats vicious Jap any day.

Whenever Bunny or I had to take a crap, we were allowed to jump into the sea to relieve ourselves. The Japs placed a rope ladder over the side of the boat, which we used to climb back in. We had to float around in a seated position of sorts until the urge to poop hit. After we'd pushed out whatever needed to come out, and after the little brown turds—or brown eyed mullets, as Bunny called them—surfaced and bobbed around us, the Japs would let us swim for a few minutes to get some exercise.

Sometimes they even jumped in with us and goofed around. After a few times, the whole experience became surreal. With all the laughter and horseplay going on between us, it was almost as if war wasn't raging around us, as if we weren't hated enemies but were instead, adventurous boys out for fun. Then it happened.

Late in the afternoon of the third day, two of the friendlier Jap guards jumped into the clear water with me and Bunny. The boat's engines had been shut off for safety reasons and the four of us swam around tossing an old coconut back and forth as if it were a baseball.

Bunny and I didn't know their names—in fact we didn't know any of the guards' names—and these two didn't speak a word of English. Probably no more than eighteen or nineteen, they just smiled a lot and laughed incessantly at almost everything we said.

Just before we were about to climb back onto the boat Bunny pulled me aside. "Throw the coconut over that one Jap's head," he whispered and jutted his chin to the left, indicating the guard he was talking about, "so he has to swim out a bit, toward the front of the boat to get it. Then get out of the water as quickly as you can."

"Why?"

Bunny rolled his eyes. "Just do it now."

"Okay." I shrugged then hurled the beaten up coconut well above the guard's outstretched arms. He turned toward the bow of the ship and started swimming to retrieve it.

Coconut in hand, he began to swim back toward the boat.

Bunny and I had already climbed safely out of the water and were stepping onto the boat.

The guard made a sound, like a groan, then stopped swimming and seemed to grab his side. A moment later, he resumed swimming and soon he and the other guard were also back onboard.

"What was that all about?" I whispered to Bunny.

He nodded toward the water on the left side of the boat, near the bow. "Didn't you see them?"

"See what?" I narrowed my gaze and stared. All I saw was water.

"Those tiny jellyfish floating by." He raised his arm and it seemed like he was about to point at something, but then he scratched his hand and a second later his hand fell back to his side.

I noticed a commotion among the guards.

The guard who'd retrieved the coconut pressed his palm against his side and grimaced. A few minutes later, covered in sweat but deathly pale, he collapsed, writhing in apparent agony. His arms and legs twitched and contorted into hideous positions. He vomited twice in a matter of seconds.

Bunny smirked.

I jabbed Bunny's side with my elbow. How could he laugh at a time like this? "What gives?" I asked in a low voice.

"Irukandji is what gives, mate. They're the most venomous marine stingers known to man, and they're no bigger than your thumb. I used to see them all the time floating in the waters north of Manly Beach. They fire tiny stingers at their prey just like poisonous missiles or, more appropriately for this wonderful occasion, poisonous darts from a blow pipe."

"You mean you deliberately sent the poor sap into a pod of poisonous jellyfish?"

"Well, actually you did, mate, when you threw that coconut over his head."

"But you . . . ." I sighed. "Can you save him?"

"I could, but I won't. This one's for Unka and the others." He turned away and moved toward the dying boy.

After forty very long minutes, the horrific struggle ended.

Bunny walked to the front of the ship and perched himself directly over the bow, his right hand holding onto a metal wire for balance. A strong sea breeze blew his hair across his face. "Slits, slits, slits," he chanted quietly in perfect imitation of Unka.

Below him, playful dolphins frolicked in the wake generated by the boat's bow as we steamed directly into the reddish-orange rays of the setting sun.

Chapter Twenty-Five

On the morning of 21 July, 1945, we arrived at the port of Kuching. It was by far the largest and most populated place I had seen in all of Borneo. The Jap guards ordered us down to our knees. Bunny and I were blindfolded and our hands were tied behind us. After a bit of manhandling, we wound up in what seemed like the back of yet another flatbed truck.

The drive took nearly an hour. Eventually the truck slowed before coming to an abrupt stop that jolted me into Bunny's side. He and I were forced off the truck and made to kneel once again, this time into a mire of soupy mud that smelled like shit.

When the blindfold was removed, I got my first glimpse of Hell.

The Batu Lintang Prisoner of War camp had originally been constructed by the Sarawak government in early 1941 to house the 2nd Battalion of the 15th Punjab regiment of the British Indian army. Now it belonged to the Imperial Japanese Army and they were using it as a prisoner of war camp.

"Bow down before your superiors!" a Japanese officer shouted in broken English.

Bunny and I lowered our heads until our noses were almost in the mud.

"Lower, pigs!" He stamped his boot on the back of my neck and pushed my entire face into the filthy sludge. "Never ever make eye contact with a samurai warrior. Do you understand?"

He moved his foot off of my neck and I lifted my head just enough to suck in a deep breath. Head still bowed, eyes downcast, I nodded.

The soldier pounded both of us in the back of our heads, most likely with the butt of his rifle. I wasn't about to look up and confirm my assumption.

As we lay injured, face down again in what was a mixture of shit and urine and dirt, four other Japanese guards dragged us by our arms into the camp.

Out of the corner of my eye, I saw two tall, blonde priests holding up large crucifixes as we were hauled past them.

The Japs deposited us like trash in front of a wooden barracks. As Bunny and I slowly regained our composure a group of prisoners rushed forward to assist us.

"You blokes okay?" one of the men asked. His voice was accented in the same way as Bunny's.

We nodded and swiped at the mess on our faces.

"Take them into the back room and get them cleaned up," an Aussie captain ordered. "Get them over to Smitty's as soon as possible."

Bunny and I were moved into the building and given a damp cloth, albeit a filthy one, with which to wipe our faces. Several of the prisoners set about tending to our wounds.

Our medical treatment was in many ways sadistically comical as the captives didn't have any real medical supplies. It basically consisted of having cleaner wet rags applied to the back of our aching heads. We were given some fruit, crackers, and a tiny bit of water and were allowed to rest for a few minutes.

Our caretakers soon helped us to our feet. "Time to meet Barracks Master Colonel R.M. Smythe and his staff. Off you go now, lads," one of them said as he walked us to toward another longhouse.

I entered the main room, hoping against hope that salvation awaited. In an instant I knew that it was not to be. In fact, I was more than convinced that if there ever was a time to abandon all hope, it was now.

Colonel Smythe and his staff, surely gaunt scarecrows of their former selves, sat behind a table in the middle of the long hallway. None of them wore a complete military uniform and more than half of them only wore loin cloths over their privates. The men were barefoot and none of them appeared to have had a decent meal in years. This grim council looked eerily like skeletons who hadn't yet realized that they had died.

Colonel Smythe slowly rose and stepped in front of the table. "Welcome to hell friends, I'm Colonel R.M. Smythe, but you can just call me Smitty like everyone else does. I'm in charge of this little compound of several longhouses. They're ten more compounds like this in our sector, each with its own barracks commander. There are several more sectors."

"Where exactly are we?" I interrupted.

"We'll clue you in on everything mate, don't you worry. But first what news do you fellas have from the outside? Rumor has it that MacArthur has recaptured the P.I. and that the Yanks have started bombing the Japanese home islands. Is this true?"

I confirmed that the P.I. had been retaken by MacArthur but told Smitty that I hadn't heard anything about an invasion of the Japanese islands.

"How'd you know about the recapture of the P.I.?" I asked.

He didn't answer. He just looked over at me and nodded. "Alright men, everyone out." I turned to leave. The Colonel's hand dropped upon my shoulder. "No, you and your friend stay.

"Have a seat on the floor." Smitty pointed to an area of the floor where what had to be about a gallon of dirt, sand mostly, was mounded up into a neat little pile. He plopped onto the floor himself and began smoothing out the dirt with his index finger. "What say we get to know each other a little," he said. "Let's start with your names."

"You can call me Bunny and this here's Flyer."
Bunny said as he put his arm around my shoulder. He filled
in the details about who we were and how we'd come to
find ourselves in the POW camp.

"Z-force, huh? And a Yank flyer. Frankly, I'm
surprised you're still alive. I'd have expected the Japs
would have pulled out all the stops torturing you fellas for
info. Very curious that they haven't done so yet."

Smitty stood up and paced in front of us. After a
moment, he picked up a pitcher of something and tossed
coconut halves to each of us.

"Hold 'em still," he said. He poured a small
measure of dark liquid into each coconut shell.

"Drink up, men. Nothing like homemade termite
juice to cure what ails you."

Bunny sniffed the liquid. "What is it?"

"Oh, just some tea the locals call 'God's Flesh'
because they say it makes them feel so good. We call it

termite juice because it's made from termite mushrooms that grow everywhere around Kuching. Drink up. It will relax you."

"Are you having any?" I asked, suddenly wary.

"Maybe later." Smitty smiled and tipped his hand toward his mouth in a drinking motion.

Bunny and I stared at each other a moment. He finally brought the shell to his lips and drained it.

I reluctantly drank my own cupful.

"That's good, boys. Now stretch out here." He patted the ground. "Make yourselves comfortable. This is going to take a while and you may as well relax."

Smitty sat next to us and, with his palm, smoothed the sand across a small space until it resembled a miniature beach. "I'm about to explain everything you need to know about Batu Lintang and how to survive it.

"What's with the sand," Bunny asked.

"I need to do a lot of drawing and we have very little paper. Besides, I can destroy this drawing in a flash." Smitty swept away a part of the beach, revealing the floor beneath.

I nodded. "Clever."

"That we are, mate, among our many other talents." Smitty grinned and began drawing in the sand. When he was finished, the shape resembled a fat potato. "Here's an aerial view of thirty or so acres of this pig sty. Three roads define most of the perimeter." He pressed his index finger into the sand and made a divot. "This large building on the outside of the gate is where the Jap officers and guards live. Lieutenant Colonel Hatori Mesuga runs the show. In fact, he's in charge of all the Jap POW camps on Borneo, so he's not here that often. He's a real pig of a man. You can't say much around him because he speaks perfect, unaccented English, like a Yank." Smitty looked at me and frowned.

I shuddered. That wasn't good. Language barriers could often be beneficial at certain times. And anyway, how could someone who'd probably grown up in the US serve in the Japanese army? Why that was about as un-American as anyone could get.

Smitty turned his attention back to his map. "When he's gone, his sadistic second in command, Captain Hideo Tagata, is in charge. He's an absolute sociopathic asshole. He's so brutal we call him the Bonecracker. He introduced himself to you earlier when he smashed your heads with the butt of his rifle.

"We've given many of the Japs nicknames so they don't know we're talking about them. The Bonecracker earned his sobriquet because he always carries a long ball-peen hammer instead of the typical Japanese Kendo stick. He's bashed many a prisoner with that bloody mallet, often starting with their toes in order to hobble them. With any new infraction—and sometimes an infraction is a simple as breathing too loudly or sneezing—the Bonecracker works his way up a prisoner's leg. You'll never be able to forget the sound of the hammer when it slams into someone's shin bone."

I winced. That was a sound I hoped I'd never have to hear.

Smitty barely seemed to notice my discomfort. Bunny's face remained stoic, not unlike that of Smitty's. I needed to toughen up or I wasn't going to make it another day here. I tried to mimic their looks of bland indifference.

"Here's a few other nicknames you'll need to learn," Smitty said a moment later. "Every morning you'll see this dumpy guard who is charge of feeding us. He fills a pig trough with boiled rice. Just before he doles out our daily allotment—a mere four ounces, by the way—he lifts up his right leg and farts on the rice. In broken English he yells, 'Okay, eat up yum-yum time.' Because he does this every single day, he's called Shitz-n-giggles."

"That's a good one," I said trying to match my mood to Smitty's, who suddenly sounded whimsical.

"Yeah. Another one assigned to police our compound we call Heshe."

Bunny raised his brows. "Why?"

"Well, because he's kind of an extremely effeminate nip. A real sissy boy, if you know what I mean." Smitty chuckled then blew air through his lips, vibrating them into a farting sound. "He . . . She. We don't really know if he's a he or a she, so we call him Heshe."

"Ah, I see," Bunny said, chuckling.

"Even funnier though," Smitty snickered, "the nip thinks 'Heshe' is our feeble attempt to speak some sort of Japanese!"

Smitty told us about many more guards, regaling us with tales of their behavior and supplying us with their nicknames before he returned to his map.

"Here." He pointed. "Just inside the front gate you fellas were dragged through is where a few dozen Dutch and Irish priests live. They were captured during the fall of Singapore and Borneo. The small hut behind the priests' housing is the chapel." Smitty marked the area in the sand.

"The women's barracks are directly on the other side of camp." Smitty drew a small building on the place he'd indicated. "We figure around two hundred fifty women live there. More than half of them are nuns and the rest are wives of male civilians located elsewhere in the camp. We've counted close to three dozen little ones there, all under the age of ten.

"Jesus," I said. "This is a hell of a place for a kid to grow up."

Smitty frowned. "No kidding. Doc Edwards, the Allied camp doctor, says that the severe malnutrition has caused most of the younger women to stop having their monthlys. With any luck, we won't have too many babies born in this hell hole."

Smitty drew another line straight across the camp, indicating where a second barbed-wire fence was located. "This is what separates them from us. Don't ever go near this fence," he warned. "The only time you get to cross to the other side is to assist with funerals."

"Does that happen often?" I asked.

"The camp averages about two a day. When a prisoner dies, the Japs select prisoners to prepare the body and serve as pall bearers. The cemetery is located just outside of the main fence and over to the left." Smitty drew an 'X' on the spot. "We call it Boot Hill."

"The Japs used to give us simple wooden coffins, but now, with all the shortages, they only allow us to wrap the bodies in burlap rice sacks or used-up blankets. After the nuns and priests protested this disrespectful burial practice, the Japs gave us a coffin with a trap door hinged at the bottom. This allows the body to be transported through the camp in a more dignified manner. Once it's directly positioned over the grave, the trap door is released and the body falls into the ground."

My heart flip flopped at the insane inhumanity of it all. Why would anyone think this was a proper way to treat people, even enemy combatants? Seconds passed as I pondered everything before I realized that Smitty was still talking.

"Farther inside the camp," Smitty's stick moved over top of the map, "are four hundred or so civies and roughly fourteen hundred Allied prisoners. You'll find thirty longhouse barracks here, each housing from thirty to a hundred prisoners. We've got blokes in here from all over. They're even a couple of other yanks around. Most prisoners, however, are Australian, British, or Dutch."

"Shit holes, literal ones this time and not the buildings in which we live, are located at the end of each of the barracks. They're holes cut into the wooden platform for you to squat over and do your business. Your shit falls into a big oil drum. On occasion, you'll be asked to clean these out. No pun intended, but it's truly a shitty job despite the fact that you'll rarely see a real turd."

"Come again, mate?" Bunny said.

"Almost every POW suffers from bloody dysentery—not all that surprising given that we're expected to live on a meager ration of four ounces of boiled rice and a few sips of fetid swamp water each day." Smitty sighed. "I tell you what, things are bad all over boys, really bad."

"The one good in all of this is that the sanitary health benefits force us to move the waste as far away from camp as possible. And once outside the gate, well, who knows what might possibly happen?" Smitty's tone sounded minutely lighter than it had a second before, though he continued to frown.

I shook my head. "This is all so unbelievable. How can the Japs get away with this treatment?"

Smitty shrugged. "They do what they want to do, what they know they can get away with."

"Don't you get any Red Cross parcels to help out?" Bunny asked.

Smitty laughed then rolled his eyes, his face becoming filled with frustration. "In the three years I've been a prisoner here, we've received exactly one Red Cross package—that was back in the summer of '44. It contained an ancient Gramaphone, one tin of sardines, some stale crackers, and a hundred or so empty tins. Obviously, the Japs busted into the parcel and stole everything of value. They re-wrapped the box as some type of sadistic joke."

"They're truly some sick little fuckers," I said.

"You don't know the half of it." Smitty looked at Bunny and me. "Never ever make eye contact with any Japanese guard. When addressed, bow down like this." He stood up and bowed deeply from his waist until his upper body was at a forty five degree angle with his legs. "You stay like that until you are told to rise. They might make you hold the position for a few seconds or for an hour or longer. We never know how it will go. If you fail to do any of this, they will beat the living shit out of you. Understand?"

Bunny and I nodded, though I would never understand how human beings could be this cruel to their own kind.

After another round of termite juice, which Smitty partook of this time around, he continued to educate us about the camp. He told us that many of the camp guards were actually Korean military conscripts. "I imagine most of them probably hate the Japs as much as we do, but their livelihoods depend on serving their Jap masters. In the presence of the Jap officers, the Korean guards perform their villainous roles to absolute perfection. But, when the

Japs are out of sight, the Koreans operate a black market operation right under the Japs' noses." He laughed.

"Everyone jokes that the Koreans are really more entrepreneur than enemy. Prisoners can get just about anything they need or want but always at an incredibly high price."

"What form of currency you talking, here?" Bunny asked.

"Gold. That's all they will take. A gold ring, for instance, might get you some medicine or might buy a chance for a man to see his wife if she's housed in the women's camp. Sadly, conditions had become so desperate that I've directed Doc Edwards to inspect every dead prisoner's mouth. If there's any gold to be had there, he knows to extract what he can."

"Even though he uses a small hammer and needle-nosed pliers, the task of removing a tooth is always a bloody and messy affair. Nonetheless, Doc has to pull the gold-filled teeth with absolute care and precision, making sure that he didn't damage a prisoner's face. We can't let the Japs know what he's doing."

One can only absorb so much horrific knowledge before the mind begins to close off and beg for mercy. My eyelids began to droop and, before I know it, closed completely.

"Hey, mate," Smitty said as he lightly smacked at my face. "Pay attention. I'm trying to save your bloody life. Oh, never mind. You're tired and I'm on edge. Let's call it quits for now. Get some rest. You fellas can stay here for the rest of the evening and in the morning we'll finish up and get you settled into your own space within this building."

Sounded good to me. Within no time, I was fast asleep.

Smitty woke us up before sunrise to instruct us about morning revelry. A half hour later the Japanese national anthem blared from the tinny loudspeaker system strung throughout the camp. The Japs were no doubt playing their national anthem on the stolen gramophone.

"Look alive, boys," Smitty said as he clapped me on the back. "It's show time."

We rushed out of the barrack with the other prisoners. Soon, every man from every longhouse had stumbled into the central compound and all of us were lined up for roll call.

"Good God," Bunny whispered, "look at these poor bastards. Most of 'em are little more than barely breathing corpses."

Sadly I had to agree. Of the hundreds of men I could see, not one of them seemed to weigh more than one hundred fifty pounds at best. Beaten down, bedraggled, and malnourished, many of them swayed while trying to remain at attention. Some looked to be so hopelessly weak that their comrades had them sandwiched in, between other slightly stronger prisoners who could hold them up.

I felt uneasy. Surely it wouldn't be long before one of these pathetic men fell out of line and the Japs set about beating him like Smitty had warned us they would.

I tried to keep from looking at my fellow prisoners. I focused on the view right in front of me and Bunny and I stood at the end of the front line. Smitty and his staff stood at attention in the center of the line about ten feet in front of everyone else. They were positioned facing us, with their backs to the Japs.

After standing at attention for a couple of minutes a commotion began from somewhere off to my left. Despite the warning to keep our eyes facing forward at all times, Bunny glanced in the direction of the sound. He did so, not by turning his head but by merely rotating his eyes toward the sound.

Instantly, a ball-peen hammer smashed into Bunny's left knee. The Bonecracker had struck without warning.

Bunny shrieked and crumpled onto the ground.

I reached toward him, thinking to offer assistance.

One of the guards rammed his rifle into my shoulder blade and I fell to my knees, next to Bunny.

The Bonecracker kicked me in the stomach with one of his steel-toed boots. I clutched my stomach while trying not to puke and rolled onto my back.

Grinning evilly, the Bonecracker raised his hammer above me.

"Tagata, stop!" a voice bellowed from across the compound. For some reason, Lieutenant Colonel Mesuga had ordered the Bonecracker to stop the attack.

"Enough!"

A couple of Jap guards ran over to where Bunny and I laid writhing in pain. They grabbed us by our arms and dragged us before Mesuga. When I looked up, I saw a short fat little man in a well ironed white uniform adorned with medals. An antiquated pith helmet adorned his head.

A pith helmet for God's sake? What a cocky little fuck.

His face was a puffy moon-shaped ball of pock-marked disdain. A permanent smirk contorted his mouth, revealing dingy yellow teeth hidden behind thick rubbery lips. He looked continuously perturbed, as if he were being forced to smell something putrid or all eternity.

"Where are you from in America?" the man asked me in perfect English.

Smitty had been right, Mesuga didn't have the slightest hint of an accent.

Still dazed, I remained silent.

"I'm a graduate of Georgetown University Class of 1919," he said, sounding proud of his alma mater. "Are you familiar with my great school? We beat both Virginia Tech and Navy that year. I used to love going to your American football games. My friends and I would get so excited we'd shout out '*Hoya Sax*' at the top of our lungs! You feel okay now, GI?"

Fearing another beating I kept my eyes downcast and slowly nodded yes.

"Good," he said. "You take your friend back to Colonel Smythe's hut for now." Mesuga directed some of the Korean guards to assist us back to Smitty's longhouse.

Chapter Twenty-Six

"I specifically told you blokes always to look straight ahead, didn't I?" Smitty said through his clenched jaw, when we were back inside.

"Sorry sir," I replied.

"Sorry? It's your second day here and look at what you've gotten yourself into. Mesuga now knows who you are, Bunny's probably crippled for life, and both of you have risen to the very top of the Bonecracker's shit list." He ran his fingers through his thinning hair and looked at Bunny. "Christ."

He motioned to a couple of his crew. "Help Bunny up. Doc needs to look at his leg straight away."

By the time Doc Edwards saw Bunny's knee it had swollen to twice its normal size. The best Doc could determine was that it probably was shattered beyond repair. He said he could feel shards of fractured bone moving underneath the skin.

Later that night I met with one of the Korean guards and traded him a small bit of gold that one of Smitty's men had given me for a bit of morphine. Unfortunately, he wasn't going to be able to get the morphine until later the next day, which meant that Bunny would have to suffer through the night in agony. The only pain relief Doc Edwards could provide came from a couple of aspirins and half a gallon of termite juice.

"Get him drunk," Doc said.

I held Bunny's hand throughout the night as he moaned and cried. He finally passed out a couple of hours before dawn.

The horrible task of waking Bunny for morning revelry fell to me. I gently shook his shoulder. "Bunny, you gotta get up. I'll help you get outside for roll call."

"I can't," he said, tears welling in his eyes. "I just can't do it today, mate."

"You have to, man. There's no other way." I snuck a quick look at his leg. The swelling hadn't subsided at all but the bleeding had stopped. A crust of dried blood still covered the area of impact. It wasn't yet a scab. Movement likely would crack it open again. But that was the least of my worries. He was never going to be able to put weight on his leg.

With an old rag and two sticks, I fashioned a crude bandage and splint to stabilize his knee. Bunny screamed from the slight pressure that resulted from the knot I tied to secure the rag in place.

"No, don't touch me," Bunny begged. "Just let me be."

"I can't do that." I nodded at some of the men who looked on. "A little help here. Let's get him to his feet."

When Bunny was fully upright he wailed, tears and snot running a race toward the floor. "Hurts like a sonofabitch, nonstop throbbing. Please lay me down. Oh, God, please put me down." Thankfully, it didn't appear that the wound had started to bleed again.

Braced by two of us supporting all of Bunny's weight under the armpits, we were able to drag him outside. We moved to the back row, as far away from Mesuga and the Bonecracker as we could possibly position ourselves. Bunny was then sandwiched between me and a big Aussie fella who'd help get him outside. We had to move our hands out from under Bunny's armpits and put them down by our sides.

I prayed that Bunny wouldn't collapse.

Lt. Col. Mesuga soon appeared.

I felt Bunny take a deep breath and lift his head up. He stared straight ahead and didn't move a bit. So far, so good.

When the Japs forced us to bow to the Emperor Hirohito, Bunny stumbled forward ever so slightly, almost bumping the man in the line in front of him.

Shit.

An instant later, we rose up from bowing and focused our eyes straight ahead.

Bunny had done it. He hadn't collapsed.

The Bonecracker shouted something I couldn't understand and rushed toward us. He entered the area between our line and the one in front of us and then slowed his steps as he neared us. When he arrived at the spot where we stood, Tagata turned toward Bunny.

Now directly face to face and no more than two inches away, he stared wildly into Bunny's eyes. Then without warning, he reached down and squeezed Bunny's mangled knee.

Bunny cried out and then collapsed onto the ground.

I tried not to react. I kept my eyes looking straight ahead.

A handful of Japanese guards quickly appeared and dragged Bunny's limp body into a small building near the front of the camp.

Oh, God. What had just happened? Would I ever see Bunny again?

Chapter Twenty-Seven

When we were dismissed I rushed to Smitty as quickly as I could. "What's going on?"

"*Kempeitai* is what is going on. I just hope Bunny is clean, that's all," Smitty said.

"Clean? What do you mean clean?"

"Clean, you know. That he doesn't have any dirt on him, like evidence tying him to Z-force, because if they find out he's a commando, those sons of bitches will do anything to get info out of him."

I soon discovered that the *Kempeitai* was the Jap equivalent of the Gestapo. Located in Kuching, the *Kempeitai* were notorious among the Sarawak people. Hell, they were infamous throughout all of Japan's so-called *Greater East Asia Co-Prosperity Sphere*, known primarily for their violent and brutal interrogation methods. In fact, the hated Jap Prime Minister Tojo—four-eyed little cock sucker that he was—had served as the *Kempeitai* overlord in Manchuria from 1935 to 1937, and everyone knew about the horrific atrocities they had committed there.

If the *Kempeitai* discovered that Bunny was a Z-force commando, it was a done deal. He would be tortured ASAP. The best I could hope for was that Bunny might conjure up some semi-believable story as to what he was doing in Borneo and why he was captured with a Dayak headhunter carrying a severed Jap soldier's head. It certainly wasn't promising.

That day and the next dragged by without the return of Bunny. I half expected the Japs to come for me at any time. By the third day, I was tormented with worry and heartsick over what might have already happened to Bunny.

Later in the afternoon, just before sunset, the Japs ordered all the prisoners under Smitty's command to assemble outside of the barracks. Nothing like this had ever happened before according to Smitty. Everyone was distressed. Not long after we came to attention, a black 1938 Chrysler pulled up in front of us.

As the big black car idled in a low, deep-down mechanical hum, the back door opened. A second later, Bunny was shoved out. None of us moved as he tumbled onto the ground.

Inside the sedan, Lt. Colonel Mesuga and Captain Tagata stared at us, both smiling ever so slightly. A second later, Tagata pulled the door shut and the car sped away. Dust and sand swirled around Bunny, who hadn't moved.

Had they just returned his corpse to us?

Aside from the fact that his head had been completely shaved, Bunny otherwise looked the same. His knee was still bruised and swollen.

We ran to him.

Exhilaration flooded my body when I saw the slow but regular rise and fall of his chest with each shallow breath. Praise the Lord. Bunny was alive.

"Well, look who's returned three days later just like the resurrected Christ!" I said as I helped him to sit.

He didn't smile or respond.

Smitty and I put our hands under his arms and carefully stood him upright. He slowly swayed back and forth in a daze, seemingly trying to balance on his one good leg. Bunny stared straight ahead, tears streamed down his cheeks. Then he moved his head cautiously from side to side and then up toward the sky. He began to blink rapidly as if he was trying to blink his way back into reality.

"What is it?" I said. "What happened?

He turned toward me and opened his mouth.

I gasped, put my hand over my mouth and recoiled.

The mother fuckers had cut out a large portion of his tongue.

I reached out and pulled him close, enveloping him in a gentle consoling embrace while he sobbed.

"Who did this to you?" I whispered after he had regained some measure of composure.

Bunny pointed to his injured knee.

"Bonecracker?"

He nodded.

"Was anyone else involved?"

Again he nodded but then he sat down and began writing in the dirt with his index finger.

M-e-s-u-g-a.

Unhinged, and hell bent on exacting bloody revenge on Mesuga and Tagata, I took off running toward the Jap guards strung out along the barbed wire fence that separated us from my targets.

They raised their weapons in my direction.

A few of Smitty's men jumped on top of me and dragged me to the ground. After a furious struggle, I calmed down just enough to realize the futility of my plan. The guards would have gunned me down long before I ever posed any real threat to them and I'd never have had a chance to murder the monster officers who had maimed my friend.

Maybe not today. But someday I would avenge my friend's suffering, even if it cost me everything, including my own life.

Over the next few days Bunny languished about the camp in a sort of angry, disillusioned stupor. Whenever I attempted to speak with him he simply scribbled notes that said things like, "I'm tired now," or "I'll catch you later." He spent pretty much every day after his return lying on a rattan mat underneath the shade of one of the few rubber trees still standing in our section of the camp. Batu Lintang had been constructed on an old rubber plantation. Most of the trees had been cut down when the camp was built but a few remained, toward the back of the compound.

I approached Bunny one afternoon without him seeing me. When I got close enough that he noticed me, he shoved something under some large banana leaves that had fallen on the ground next to him.

I wasn't about to ask him what he was apparently hiding, but whatever it was, he didn't want me or anyone else to see it.

Curiosity however, got the better of me later that day.

Bunny had moved back to his pallet in the longhouse. I returned to the place where I'd seen him stash something. The banana leaves were still scattered on the ground. I glanced around to see if anyone was looking at me. When it seemed that I was alone and unwatched, I casually brushed the leaves away with my foot, sweeping them toward the tree trunk.

Nothing lay underneath them and the ground appeared intact with no evidence that it had recently been dug up and then repacked.

What a little shit I'd become, violating my friend's privacy like that. Head down, I slunk away.

Chapter Twenty-Eight

Because I was a healthy prisoner, relatively speaking, I was assigned to various work details over the next week. On 1 August, 1945, I was one of two dozen prisoners placed on trucks and taken to work in the timber yards, located on the outskirts of Kuching. The Jap guards who watched us when we were taken outside of the camp were especially vicious.

Two days later, the work detail was taken to a small Jap airfield about five miles from Batu Lintang. There the Japs put us to work refueling airplanes. This was probably not a good idea because, whenever the guards weren't looking, we pissed in the airplane's fuel tanks. When we'd completely drained our bladders, we'd put sand into the tanks. At night, back at camp, we laughed as we imagined the clueless Zero pilot frantically trying to figure out why he was about to crash into the South China Sea.

All prisoners who worked for the Japs were paid twenty five cents per day for their services. Although this was a direct violation of the 1907 Hague Convention, most prisoners were happy to get money with which they purchased medicine or food such as frogs, snakes, snails, or rat meat from the local Chinese merchants who occasionally were allowed into camp.

I came to a worrisome conclusion on the fourth of August. I'd only resided in Batu Lintang for fourteen days, but already my body was starting to break down from malnutrition. Unbelievably, I even craved Sago worms and rice and would have given my left nut for a large bowl of them.

On that same day, I realized something else, something that I hadn't picked up on during my first two weeks in hell. Something strange, perhaps even sinister, was going on in camp.

Whereas almost every prisoner looked decrepit, diseased, and malnourished, one particular group of prisoners within our compound of longhouses seemed to be flourishing. This group of men, an odd assortment of Australians and British soldiers, lived separately in barracks headed up by Lieutenant Emery Winsborough.

Winsborough was known throughout the camp solely by his nickname "Sparks." Apparently, he'd been some sort of electrical guru back in Australia. Not only were Sparks and his men extremely well preserved, but they always seemed to be in close proximity to Colonel Smythe and his staff.

I eventually confronted Smitty about Sparks and his mystery men later that evening.

Smitty skillfully deflected my questions and quickly changed the subject. Before I knew it, he'd pretty much dismissed me by telling me to go get some sleep.

More suspicious than ever, I nevertheless realized that I wasn't going to get the info I wanted from Smitty. I forced myself to walk away from him, keeping my demeanor cool, calm, and matter of fact. If he wouldn't tell me what was going on, I'd find out some other way.

Shortly after sunrise on Sunday, August 5th, the prisoners of Col. R.M. Smythe's barracks shuffled outside for what we thought was to be another typical morning roll call, made different only by the fact that it was Sunday and Lieutenant Colonel Mesuga and Captain Tagata would personally inspect each prisoner like they did every Sunday. This up-close, literally in-your-face, invasion of our personal space was their way of further intimidating us. Everyone was on edge.

Bunny, now barely able to walk because of his mangled knee limped toward his assigned place.

"Are you okay?" I asked.

He didn't respond but it was obvious that he dreaded this inspection.

Over the past few days Bunny had been absolutely unbearable to live with. He didn't speak, he didn't eat, and he didn't drink. He just lay like a decomposing corpse under his banana tree or on his indoor pallet and moved only when he had to. It killed me to see Bunny like this and saddened me that he wouldn't let me in after all we'd been through.

I moved myself in front of him when we'd reached our place in line. "What in the hell is the matter with you?" As I stared at Bunny, looking straight into his blank eyes, clarity struck. Bunny had given up. He was just going through the last motions he needed to go through before he died.

Grimacing, he shifted his weight off of his bad leg.

"Is something going on with your knee?" I whispered. "Why are you limping so badly?"

Mesuga and Tagata approached the back line where we were. I heard Bunny take in a long deep breath. As soon as Mesuga and Tagata got within just a few feet of where we were, Bunny mumbled something with his mangled tongue that I couldn't understand. At the same time, he reached down into his heavily bandaged knee and extracted a long bamboo shiv with a ferocious looking point.

He lunged at Tagata with a vicious upward thrust, trying to stab him beneath his chin.

The Bonecracker turned his head just in time. The shiv missed its mark and merely sliced open his left cheek.

Blood spurting from his facial wound, the Bonecracker raised his ball-peen hammer over his head then slammed it into Bunny's forehead.

Bunny collapsed as the Bonecracker stumbled backward.

A few of the prisoners jumped between Bunny and the Bonecracker to prevent further violence. By then the Jap guards had entered the fray and quickly restored order.

Mesuga ordered the guards to drag Bunny's limp body into the center of the compound and to assemble the rest of us there. He jumped on top of a crate and stared us down. "How dare you attack an officer of the Imperial Army," he screamed in perfect English. "This behavior shall not, will not, and cannot be tolerated!"

He instructed some of the guards to get Bunny on his feet and bind his arms and legs with rope. Then he said something to Tagata that seemed to amuse the man.

The Bonecracker scurried toward the barbed wire area, behind which was the officers' headquarters. When he returned a few minutes later, he held up the garrote for everyone to see. The old fashioned French killing device was made up of two brass handle grips connected by nearly two feet or so of industrial strength wire.

A barely conscious Bunny was positioned in front of us, held up by two short but well-muscled Japanese guards. By this time more Japanese and Korean guards had poured into the compound, their bayonet affixed guns leveled directly at us

The Bonecracker moved behind Bunny.

"This is a war crime!" Smitty yelled out to Mesuga. "You will be held accountable!"

"Not likely," Mesuga smirked as he flicked his finger toward Tagata. "Do it."

The Bonecracker pounced, throwing the wire over Bunny's head and yanking it tightly around his neck. Bunny's face reddened and his arms flailed out. But he was so weak and nearly unconscious that he offered up no real resistance.

I lunged forward in a feeble attempt to free Bunny, but was quickly driven back by the Jap guards and their bayonets.

Tagata had pulled the wire so tight around Bunny's neck that Bunny's feet lifted off the ground and kicked in that same ineffectual way that his arms had flailed. After what seemed to be an eternity, Bunny's struggle finally ended and his broken body went limp.

The Bonecracker loosened the garrote.

Bunny sagged toward the ground then crumpled face first into the dirt, dead.

Weapons leveled at us, Mesuga, Tagata and the guards backed out of our compound.

"You'll pay for this, you bloody bastard," Smitty yelled as they continued their retreat.

Mesuga smirked again. "I doubt it." He and the rest of his men fled through the gate, back to their safe place behind the barbed wire.

One of the Australians quickly retrieved a blanket from the barracks and covered Bunny's body.

Smitty pointed to a few of Bunny's mourners. "Take him into the longhouse. Put him on the big table. I'll prepare his body for the funeral."

For the next few minutes I could not move. I was numb, perhaps even in a state of shock.

Finally, on my way to the barracks, I looked at the lone rubber tree where Bunny had spent most of his last days. He must have carved the shiv there and that was what I'd seen him hide under the leaf. "Damn it Bunny," I whispered to myself as I meandered toward the tree. "You shouldn't have done it. If only you'd talked to me first."

My body shook and I couldn't think straight. How could I ever make sense of any of this? Bunny had been one of the best of the good guys. In my eyes, he'd been larger than life, and I had somehow let him down, failing to save him as he'd no doubt saved me.

I plopped down in Bunny's favorite spot, my back against his tree and tried to make sense of the senseless. A small, terrible cry burst through my lips and then I gave into it and let myself sob. I wasn't simply crying over the loss of a cherished friend, I was lamenting his absence on this earth. My suffering felt biblical. Where was God?

When the last of my tears had dried on my face, I stood up, intent on returning to the barracks and to help Smitty prepare Bunny for his funeral. Looking down one final time, I noticed several large rubber tree leaves neatly stacked, one on top of the other. I shuffled one of my feet through the leaves and felt my heart skip a beat.

Bunny had left a short note, just a few lines actually. It was scratched onto a piece of bark, written with ink that looked to be a mixture of charcoal, ash and water.

'Flyer my friend,' it began, 'don't be sad. I'm in the stars now. Look for me tonight near the Big Dipper. I'll be telling your dad all about his great son. If you make it out alive please visit my wife and kids and explain what we did in Borneo—how we lived and how we died. Figjam! Your friend, Bunny.'

Unbidden tears falling on the ground, I wailed so hard that Smitty and a few others had to come over and console me. I don't think I've ever hugged another man as tightly as I hugged Smitty. When I felt better, Smitty and the others walked me to our longhouse, each of us lost in our own thoughts.

I kept my eyes focused straight ahead as I passed by Bunny's body on the big table. I just couldn't see him that way right now. I quickly made my way to the mat where I slept.

Someone had left me a note, written in Japanese. 言語道断. The translation roughly implied that some things were so bad that no words can describe them.

Who had left this note for me? Obviously, it was someone who understood Japanese well enough to write it.

Maybe it had come from one of the guards, perhaps one of the Korean conscripts sympathetic to our suffering. None of the men who were closest to me or Bunny, seemed conversant enough in Japanese to have composed it. I laid on my mat for a while, pondering this and so many other things. Mostly my heart just ached for Bunny and for what his loss meant to me personally. Once again, a friend was dead and I wasn't. I now was quite certain, one of these days, my number would soon come up.

After resting for a few hours, Smitty appeared in front of my sleeping area. "Get up, mate. Bunny wouldn't want you to wallow and it's depressing the hell out of me and the other men in the house. Time to return to the gathering area and be with your friends."

Friends! Who needed 'em. My friend died and I couldn't go through much more of this. I shook my head and remained on the mat. "Go away."

"Not a bloody chance in hell of that happening." Smitty tugged my arm and before I knew it I was on my feet. "That's a good lad."

When we arrived at the main gathering area of the house I saw that a priest was there, sitting next to Bunny's body. "Who's that," I whispered to Smitty out of the corner of my mouth, trying not to be too obvious or disrespectful.

"Father Charles Joseph Donovan. He's an Irish missionary who was captured when Singapore fell," Smitty said. He hurried through the introductions and then told the priest about my relationship with Bunny.

"Bless you, my son," Father Donovan said. "I'm so terribly sorry for your loss."

I nodded, unwilling to speak. The last thing I wanted now was to start bawling again.

Perhaps sensing my fragile state of mind, Father Donovan urged me to sit next to him and then proceeded to tell me a little about himself. He had a beautiful, effervescent spirit about him and, like all Irishmen, he had a certain twinkle in his eye. His positive, upbeat and natural outlook on life and death was most reassuring and within moments I was feeling marginally better, well at least not on the verge of tears.

"Please call me Father Charlie, like the rest of the lads do. I insist."

I mustered up a small grin and nodded.

"They call you Flyer, do they? Well, okay then, Flyer," Father Charlie said without pause. "You see, I'm going to take care of your friend Bunny here, but I only know how to do these things one way and that's the Irish way, which, of course, is the right way, so that's why we do it that way, understand?"

"Sure," I said, although I wasn't quite sure what he really meant.

"That's the spirit. All right then. When possible, anybody who dies in this camp gets what we like to call 'the Irish send-off.' It doesn't matter if he's a bloody Hindu or Zoroastrian, everyone gets sent off the Irish way. Now I've already spoken to Mesuga, that beast of a man—may he go straight to Hell and not have a drop of port to quench his thirst or a pot to piss in—and he gave the okay for us to have our Irish wake for Bunny."

Father Charlie looked at Smitty. "Colonel Smythe here has generously donated a bit of the gold taken from the teeth of some of our dearly departed comrades and offered it to the Korean guards in exchange for some whiskey. Now everyone knows that one of the most essential parts of a real Irish wake is, first and foremost, to honor the Spirit of Barley, but don't go getting your hopes up that we'll be receiving any Old Donegal, the finest ten-year-old Irish whiskey that Dublin ever produced. Not to worry though, whatever the Koreans get us we'll certainly put to good use."

It seemed that Father Charlie had delivered all of that without even taking a breath. His enthusiasm and energy might be just what I needed now to get through this.

"Are you ready to start?" Smitty asked Father Charlie.

"Absolutely. Flyer, will you remove that blanket from in front of the window?"

"Why?" I asked.

"The window must be left open for at least a couple of hours in order to let Bunny's soul escape into the afterlife. After two hours we'll close it up to prevent your friend's spirit from returning to his body. During this time no one stands or walks between Bunny's body and the window. Understand?"

I didn't really, but I set off anyway to remove the blanket to let the late afternoon air in and Bunny's spirit out.

"What happens if someone walks between Bunny's body and the window," I asked as I moved sideways, away from the window, careful not to cross in front of Bunny's body.

"That might bring us even more bad luck than we've already had, as if that's even possible, sweet Mary and Joseph." Father Charlie then instructed us that no person was to enter the room wearing a watch and that those few wearing one now were made to remove it and stow it away. "In this room time has stopped," he proclaimed. "All mirrors are to be covered, and Bunny's remains are never to be left alone from now until the time of his burial. We won't have to worry about keening now, since it's already been done."

"Keening?" Too bad I hadn't been raised as an Irish Catholic. I had no idea what Father Charlie was yammering on about. My people back home had boring, miserably depressing funerals compared to this and we certainly didn't have so many rules, and of course nobody drank whiskey at the funeral either.

"My boy, keening is what you were doing underneath that tree for nearly three hours. It's the uncontrollable release of emotions that pour out of people when someone they dearly love has died. And from what I heard a while back, you did enough keening for ten departed souls, bless your gentle heart."

I felt my cheeks redden, but I wasn't about to apologize for my raw expression of emotion on Bunny's behalf. I only wished now that it had occurred in private.

"There now, lad," Father Charlie said as he threw his arm around my shoulder. "I was just trying to lighten the mood. My sincere apologies to you."

"No problem, it's fine." I sighed.

"All right then, Okay, your friend will be washed and blessed in the name of our Lord and Savior Jesus Christ. One of my rosaries and a small wooden crucifix will be placed on his chest and two 1930 Mercury head dimes will be placed on his eyes, because well they were the only coins I could find on such short notice."

Seth McNamara, one of the Aussie prisoners, stepped forward and dropped the dimes into my palm. "These are special dimes and I want 'em back."

"Why are they so special?" I asked.

"They were given to my uncle, who lived in New York City during the Great Depression, by none other than Mr. John D. Rockefeller."

My jaw dropped open. "Wow. He was one of the richest men in the world."

"Yes sir," Seth said.

Father Charlie cleared his throat. "I need to finish explaining things so we can get on with this wake. Okay, where was I? Oh, now I remember. Bunny's body will then be covered in a plain white sheet that we stole from the Jap's infirmary. It'll be his shroud. We'll pray a wee bit, sing a wee bit, and then dance and drink a whole lot over his remains and wait with the body until tomorrow morning. Then we'll bury him in Boot Hill. Don't worry, Yank, it'll be a fine send off."

I squeezed the dimes. "Why will you put coins on Bunny's eyes?"

Father Charlie tilted his head. "We do that so that he'll have money to pay Charon to ferry him across the river Styx."

I looked at Seth. "But, I thought you . . ."

Father Charlie laughed. "Oh, you are a gullible one, aren't you? Actually, we use the dimes to keep the deceased's eyes from popping open. I don't want to be stared at all night by a corpse. Makes me a wee bit uncomfortable. I'll give the dimes back to Seth in the morning. You see, when people die, muscle control disappears and jaws hang down, tongues flop out, and eye lids pop open. It's a most displeasing sight. Back in the old days, people sometimes tied a strip of cloth around a corpse's head to keep the jaw closed and the tongue inside. Don't you remember the ghost of Jacob Marley in Dicken's *A Christmas Carol*? It's done kind of like that."

I remembered Jacob Marley from the 1938 film *A Christmas Carol,* the one starring Reginald Owen. It was shown at the Palace Theater back home. Funny, I'd always assumed the cloth tied around his head was because he had a bad toothache or something. Go figure.

Not long after Father Charlie finished telling me about the wake, two Australians from one of the Women's Barracks and about a half a dozen Catholic priests entered our longhouse to help Father Donovan prepare Bunny's body for burial. Before any of them entered into the common area, I scanned each of their arms for signs of a watch. Satisfied that no time pieces were being brought into the room, I allowed them to enter.

Three of the priests carried musical instruments. One had what looked to be a guitar, one had a violin and the last one carried a banjo. The other priests carried large wooden crosses and a small wooden cup for communion. A few minutes later, a Korean guard showed up at the back of the longhouse and asked to speak with Father Charlie.

"Did you get it?" I overheard Father Charlie ask.

"Yes," the guard said in English. I saw him pull out three bottles from under his shirt. A moment later he was gone.

"May the Lamb of God stir his hoof through the roof of heaven and kick that ignorant yellow-skinned fool right in the arse and straight down to hell," Father Charlie bellowed.

"What's the matter?" I asked.

"That moonfaced ignoramus brought *Old Bushmill's* whiskey, blast it all. May as well have just brought us a bottle of Protestant horse-piss. What is a

Catholic priest supposed to do with this fetid and putrid concoction? This might pass as whiskey for the Orangemen, but it can hardly suffice for a true, Irish Catholic, Republican." He wailed about theatrically then uncorked the top of one of the bottles and inhaled the amber liquid.

"Oh, well, I guess it will have to do," he said with a sigh. He tipped the bottle to his lips, took a long pull then grimaced.

Before the women began preparing Bunny's body for burial, I went over to the table where he lay. I closed my eyes, said a short prayer, and promised myself that if I made it out of Batu Lintang alive, I'd honor Bunny's final request and one day return his most cherished possessions—his wedding band and that special photo—to his wife and kids and I would explain everything to them just as he asked.

I reached down and gently placed my index finger on Bunny's forehead and slowly made the sign of a cross. I carefully avoided the terrible, bloodied indentation left on his forehead by the Bonecrusher's cursed hammer. "God bless you in the name of Jesus Christ," I whispered.

After Bunny's corpse was bathed and prepared for burial the dimes were removed from his eyes and Bunny was wrapped in a clean or rather semi-clean white sheet. Father Charlie dropped the dimes back on top of where Bunny's eyes probably were. He straightened himself like an arrow pointed skyward, said a few prayers while blessing Bunny's shrouded head with the sign of the cross and then administered the appropriate last rites for the departed. He sprinkled Bunny with what he said was holy water and asked everyone in the room to bow their heads in final prayer.

"Let us now rejoice in remembrance of the life of Bunny Hobson," Father Charlie proclaimed. At that moment, the three priests who'd brought their musical instruments began playing and singing a tune that I'd never heard before.

"There was a wild colonial boy, Jack Duggan was his name. He was born and raised in Ireland in a place called Castlemaine. He was his father's only son his mother's pride and joy, and dearly did his parents love the wild colonial boy. At the early age of sixteen years he left his native home, and to Australia's sunny shore he was inclined to roam. He robbed the rich, he helped the poor, and he shot James

McAvoy. A terror to Australia was the wild colonial boy..."

While the song continued, Smitty threw his arm around my neck. "Drink up now, Flyer. You'll feel better in the morning."

I looked at him and said, "I don't think I'll ever feel better again."

"Oh, sure you will, son, just give it some time, you'll see." He clapped me on the back and turned away, heading toward one of the older Australian women. She couldn't have been a day under sixty.

"Care to dance, beautiful?" Smitty said with an exaggerated bow as he clasped her hand.

She laughed. "Certainly, handsome."

I watched Smitty and the old woman dance non-stop, one sad waltz after another, for the next forty-five minutes. Both of them looked happy, relaxed even. After being holed up in this shithole for so long, it must have felt damn good for Smitty to have a woman, any woman, close to him.

I uncorked the *Old Bushmill's*, took a long steady pull then began to choke. Father Charlie had been right. This stuff tasted like shit and boy did it ever burn going down. I had to hand it to the Irish—they certainly knew their whiskey and what tried to pass for it.

The *Old Bushmill's* was the first alcohol I'd had since I left Australia. It now seemed like forever ago that I was hanging around with the crew of *Betty Grable's Ass*, chasing around the local Australian girls and pouring down the ale with not a worry in the world. What a difference a few weeks can make.

Bunny's wake continued through the night and lasted until a few hours before dawn. I'd never seen anyone drink as much as Father Charlie did. And the craziest thing was that he never seemed to get drunk! He just kept talking and dancing and singing and drinking throughout the entire night. The man obviously had a hollow leg.

When I awoke the next morning a little before sunrise I was in pretty bad shape. My heart was filled with sadness, my head throbbed, it even hurt to breathe. I fluttered my eyelids a few times, trying to bring the world around me into focus. Pain shot throughout my body, absolutely crushing me. After a moment, things slowly began to come into focus.

Everyone else in the room was still asleep in the golden slumbers of their drunken stupors. One of the priests slept in a chair, his hair tousled about as if he'd been in a wrestling match. The older woman was asleep on the floor next to him, her blouse slightly undone. One of her thick alabaster tits had popped out and was dangling off to the side. I'm not proud of the fact that I ogled a sixty-year-old tit for close to five minutes, but I did.

Father Charlie burst into the room, breaking my lascivious trance. "All right, you bloody Langers, rise and shine with the whole lot of you," he shouted. "We've got work to tend to." He rousted the priests, shaking each of them roughly. "C'mon, get up, you filthy bunch of Irish inchers, get up!"

"What time is it?" one of the disheveled ladies asked while straightening her skirt. She was in quite a state of undress, though not as much as the older woman who'd just shoved her big jug back inside her blouse.

"Now, now, Ms. Sullivan, I never figured you to be a pony girl," Father Charlie said, tone stern. "And for the love of Mike, with one of my priest's? You get along now."

Both women quickly gathered their belongings. "I'll be speaking with you girls later, you hear?" Father Charlie waggled his index finger at them and shooed them out of the longhouse. "The rest of you fellas tend to your morning business then get outside for roll call."

After the morning assembly ended, Smitty and I, along with four of the priests who still seemed drunk, stood next to our longhouse in the overly bright sunshine of another steamy Batu Lintang morning. It wasn't even eight o'clock but the temperature had to be pushing ninety degrees.

Father Charlie gathered us into a small circle. "Okay everyone listen up. Mesuga will allow the seven of us to take Bunny to Boot Hill for burial. Some of the locals heard what happened yesterday and have already dug a fresh grave for him, along the left side wall of the cemetery. We'll put Bunny in the coffin and walk him through the compound to the front gate. The bastard's will no doubt open the coffin and pull back the shroud to make sure it's Bunny. After that, we'll be given about fifteen minutes to drop Bunny into the grave. The locals will cover him up."

Father Charlie turned to me. "If you want some type of wooden marker, the local's will make it. Smitty will pay them later. You'd better write out whatever it is you want on the marker now." He handed me a piece of paper torn from an old Japanese instructional manual, and a small nub of a pencil, with the tiniest point of lead I'd ever seen.

I scratched out the following:

George Randolph 'Bunny' Hobson

Manly Beach Australia

Killed August 5, 1945

'*I will be conquered; I will not capitulate.*'

I handed the inscription to Father Charlie. After he read it, he nodded and put it in his shirt pocket. "All right then let's get a move on before the Japs change their bloody minds."

The priests removed the dimes from Bunny's eyes and tossed them back to Seth. They hoisted Bunny's wrapped body from the table and carefully placed him in the coffin with the trap door. Smitty and I and the priests heaved the coffin up to our shoulders. We would be the pallbearers.

Father Charlie led the funeral procession through the camp. In his right hand he held up a Bible and in his left he held his rosary beads. A few of the Jap guards stood off to the side, laughing and snickering and pointing at us as we passed. Out of the corner of my eye, I saw the Bonecracker sitting shirtless on a long bench with some of his comrades. He was eating a banana just like a monkey. Just before he was finished, he began mocking us by placing his hands around his throat and making choking sounds. Pureed banana and saliva slowly spilled from his mouth and dribbled down onto his chin.

I shifted my eyes straight ahead and tried to ignore his repulsive antics. One day, perhaps soon, he would no longer laugh.

The funeral procession passed through the front gates of Boot Hill Cemetery. Above us hung a sign, written in English. It read:

'A well-spent day brings happy sleep.'

Father Charlie led us to the freshly dug grave. We positioned the coffin directly above the hole. Father Charlie said a few last words then reached underneath the coffin and unhinged the trap door. Bunny landed in the grave with a heavy thud.

I squeezed my eyes tight, took a deep breath, and pictured Bunny in better times, smiling, healthy and confident. He was gone now, but he would never be forgotten.

I opened my eyes just as Father Charlie closed the coffin's trap door. The finality of the moment made me dizzy and almost sent me tumbling into the grave alongside Bunny.

"You okay, lad?" Father Charlie steadied my swaying body with his firm grip.

I nodded.

"You'll get through this. I promise. Let's head back."

We slowly, yet somberly, returned through the gates of Batu Lintang, back into our own little slice of hell.

Chapter Twenty-Nine

Two days after Bunny's funeral, Smitty and I noticed a weird and abrupt change in the behavior of our Japanese captors. The cold, hard faces of the Jap guards now seemed etched with a sense of great concern. They no longer smiled or laughed among themselves and they had nearly stopped all unnecessary interaction with us at all. Mesuga also seemed more frenzied than usual, wearing a worried look as he barked orders nonstop. Throughout the day of August the 8th, we watched soldiers carry out armloads of papers from their headquarters and dump them into oil drums that were set afire. Toward late afternoon, heavily armed guards were sent inside the main wire and positioned in front of each of the prisoner longhouses.

Something had happened. Something big. We just didn't know what.

"Better get in touch with Mrs. Harris and find out what in the hell is going on with the Japs," Smitty said to Sparks as I rounded the corner of the longhouse late in the afternoon. They sat on the ground with their heads together.

Sparks jumped up and hurried away. I plopped myself next to Smitty.

"Mrs. Harris?" I said, raising my eyebrows.

Smitty looked at me a few long seconds then nodded. "Over here, closer."

I scooted near. "What I'm about to tell you, mate has to stay between you and me. You have to swear."

"I swear."

"If you reveal any of this to anyone, the penalty is instant death." He dragged out the last word and let it hang there between us for a moment.

"You've got my word," I said, drawing an X with my index finger over my heart.

"Only the Board of Directors knows what I'm about to tell you." Smitty leaned so close to me, I could feel his breath on the side of my face. "You see, Flyer, Mrs. Harris is not a she. She's an 'it' we created in February of '43, and boy oh boy, let me tell you, mate, she's a real beauty."

What the heck was he talking about?

Smitty must have seen my confusion but either misread it or just didn't care. "But—"

He waved me off. "Shush, Flyer. You want to hear this or not?"

"Sorry. Go on."

"Mrs. Harris, who we sometimes just call The Old Lady, is a radio that Sparks made out of a bunch of scavenged scraps." Smitty smiled proudly, looking just like a new father so pleased with himself after the birth of his first child.

"So that's how you guys knew about MacArthur recapturing the Philippines and that the Americans had begun bombing the Japanese home islands."

Smitty grinned.

"Bunny and I wondered how you fellas knew things about the outside world some of which we didn't even know."

"Yep that's right, my boy, that's exactly how we knew what was going on." Smitty chuckled.

"How on earth did you make a radio in this God forsaken wasteland?"

Smitty pursed his lips and shook his head. "It wasn't easy, that's for sure. A couple of fellas on the work details that labored outside of camp made contact with a Chinese family called the Minghs, pro-allies. They offered to assist us in procuring the parts to construct the radio. Sparks made the radio receiver from just about anything he could get his hands on; the steering damper of an old

Norton motorcycle, parts stolen from Jap automobiles, some mica and barbed wire, pieces of glass, various useable radio parts from a broken radio, and even a Bakelite shaving soap container. He built the damn thing in just over four weeks."

"But what'd you use for power?" I asked.

"At first, we used torch batteries that we smuggled in. Unfortunately, they ran out of juice too quickly. We then tapped into the camp's electrical supply via the back of the guardhouse. But that was an extremely dangerous endeavor, so we ended up powering it with our own human generator."

"What in the hell is a human generator?"

"Manpower, mate. Manpower. We made the bloody generator right under the Japs' noses and they didn't suspect a thing. Whenever they came by and saw all of our crude tools and parts lying around, we simply told them that we were repairing watches and clocks for other prisoners. In fact, we even busted up a couple of old wristwatches and scattered the parts around the table to make it look legit."

"That's absolutely brilliant, but what powered the generator?"

Smitty smiled. "I already told you, mate—humans did."

"What am I missing here?" I asked.

"Remember when you asked me about the lads living in Sparks' barrack a few days ago?"

"Sure do. You blew me off when I asked why they looked so well-fed and exceptionally fit compared to the rest of us scarecrows."

"Sorry about that, lad. I didn't mean to hurt your feelings. But you didn't need to know about any of it then. Anyway, those are the fellas who provide the generator with power. They operate just like hamsters on a wheel. Sparks determined that in order to acquire enough power for the radio to work properly we needed to get the generator to turn about three thousand revolutions per minute. We decided that only the strongest and most fit men could possibly complete this task. So we've been giving those few men extra food and provisions to build up their strength and endurance."

"Holy shit, I knew something was up when I first saw those guys strutting around looking like Charles Atlas when everyone else looked like the fucking walking dead."

"Yes, indeed," Smitty replied. "Amongst ourselves we call those fellas the *Golden Gods of Batu Lintang.*"

"Okay, I get it now. So, please tell me what's going on in the outside world."

"The Board of Directors last received information from the outside world about two weeks ago. Although the radio can be set up and broken down within forty five seconds, finding a safe moment, and more importantly the right weather conditions, to operate it in are sporadic at best. For instance, many tropical nights are too cloudy, too rainy, or too windy to get decent reception, so information from the outside, more often than not, is delayed. Hopefully tonight Sparks and his boys will be able to get good reception and provide us with details about what's got the Japs so concerned."

The night was crystal clear, not a cloud in the sky. Smiling, I looked up and studied the Big Dipper and thought of Bunny. It comforted me to imagine him up there, looking down on us, watching over things. Throughout the night, men drifted in and out of Smitty's barracks, all asking if he had any information.

The Japs had to sense our anxiety and they had to notice the hundreds of prisoners milling about, going in and out of the longhouses. This was, most certainly, not typical of any other night since I'd arrived.

Around midnight Sparks entered our barrack and approached Smitty. I was sitting at the long wooden table next to him and a few of his staff officers. It was the same table that we'd used to prepare Bunny's body for burial.

Smitty pushed his chair back from the table and stood up, looking expectant. "Well, what's the skinny, mate? Did you find out anything?"

Sparks nodded and the corners of lips turned up. His smile quickly grew enormous.

"Hiroshima."

"What is Hiroshima?" Smitty asked.

"Hiroshima was—and I emphasize WAS—an enormous Jap city located on the island of Honshu. It ceased to exist two days ago."

The room erupted into a cacophonous gabble, as each of us threw questions at Sparks. He held his palms toward us until we quieted down.

"When we started to receive transmission from the outside, much of it was muddled and sounded like some type of code. For instance we picked up fragments of words like 'Tin. . .' and 'Hiro. . .' until we properly repositioned our antennas. We also noticed that radio chatter was extremely heavy on almost all our frequencies. Eventually though, we picked up better reception and started putting things together. Apparently the Yanks detonated some type of mega bomb over the Japanese city of Hiroshima on August sixth. By all accounts, tens of thousands were killed instantly and the city's infrastructure was completely destroyed. Jap radio out of Kuching indicated this as well. It's believed that the Japs first realized this incredible annihilation when all radio contact with Hiroshima was lost. Soon after, they realized that military bases in the area couldn't be contacted either. The best I can figure at this time is that the Americans detonated some type of nuclear weapon and, if that's the case, this war will soon to be over!"

Everyone erupted again, this time with smiles and hoots and congratulatory slaps on the back.

"Is there any of that shitty *Old Bushmill's* left?" Smitty shouted at me.

"About a half a bottle," I screamed.

"Go get it and give everybody a pull," he ordered.

For the first time in weeks, I felt hopeful and, dare I say it, happy.

Throughout the rest of that night, we discretely spread the good news to other prisoners in the camp and told them to pass it on. However, as promising as this news was, the fact remained that we were still prisoners of war, held by sadistic Japs somewhere in the land that time had forgotten. Buoyed with hope but still tethered to a sinking ship, none of us knew what our immediate future held, and we were still a little afraid to let our expectations ride too high.

Three days later, on August twelfth, Sparks informed Smitty that a second mega-bomb had been dropped by the Americans, this time destroying the industrial city of Nagasaki and obliterating another eighty thousand Japs in the process.

How much longer could this Armageddon last? How much more could the Japs take? We all knew the Nips were not big on surrender based on their sacred Code of the Bushido. History offered up several stunning Allied defeats of them after which their soldiers continued to fight on even when all hope was lost. They simply would not capitulate. But were they really willing to let their women and children commit national suicide along with the soldiers all for the sake of their own stubborn pride?

Chapter Thirty

With Japan now experiencing the death throes of an empire, surviving each day in the camp became increasingly difficult. Overall conditions didn't improve in the least after Hiroshima and Nagasaki were annihilated. In fact, they got even worse.

Knowing that Japan had already lost the war but had yet to capitulate, knowing that their homes and loved ones were now most likely forever gone, the Japs guarding us turned their anger and resentment toward us. Beatings occurred frequently, food was deprived and psychological torment increased drastically.

One afternoon, for no apparent reason, Tagata entered Smitty's compound and dragged me and another prisoner outside. "Kneel, dogs," he screamed at us in heavily accented English

As other prisoners came out of their longhouses and filled the compound yard, Tagata held up his pistol and loaded one bullet into the chamber. He spun it around and around.

After a second, he pointed the gun at my head and pulled the trigger.

A hollow click sounded as the hammer slammed into an empty chamber.

Tagata laughed his sadistic laugh then aimed his gun at the head of the man next to me. Sergeant Torrey Parker was a non-descript Australian serving on Smitty's staff. He usually kept to himself and minded his own business.

"Please, no," Sergeant Parker pleaded. "Don't, please. I'm sorry, I'm sorry. Please I have a wife and kids, for Christ sake." As he attempted to stand, Tagata struck him with a fierce blow to the left side of his head. Sergeant Parker crumpled unconscious to the ground, blood covering the side of his face.

Tagata raised his revolver in the air and spun the chamber again. He grabbed Sergeant Parker by the hair, lifting his head off of the ground. The Bonecracker pointed his pistol directly into Parker's face and pulled the trigger.

Click. Again, the chamber was empty.

Tagata pulled the hammer back once more then squeezed the trigger.

Again, the only sound was a click.

"This one lucky kangaroo fucker!" Tagata screamed. He dropped Parker's head back into the dirt, stepped over his broken body, and casually walked away.

This type of sick psychological shit continued throughout the next couple of days—absolute fucking God-awful terror that seemed to have no end.

Shortly before midnight on the fourteenth of August, Sparks entered the longhouse even more animated than he'd been on the night he'd informed us about Hiroshima. "I have news," he said to Smitty, "from Jun Lei."

Jun was a Chinese Malaysian who'd majored in linguistics prior to the war. He spoke a variety of languages, one of which was Japanese. Sparks had ordered him to listen in on every radio transmission he could, and it was news from this night's transmissions that had Sparks so concerned.

"Jun believes the voice on the radio he heard," Sparks said with a pause and a deep breath, "was none other than that of Emperor Hirohito himself."

"Can't be," Smitty said. "That bastard never addresses his people. He considers himself too much a deity to speak to them directly."

"That's what I thought. But Jun assures me he heard an address by none other than the emperor himself. He had great difficulty understanding what the bastard was saying because he spoke in what Jun said was classical Japanese. Jun doubts that the average Jap citizen understood exactly what he was saying. It's kind of the same as a modern man trying to understand someone speaking old English like in the style of Shakespeare or Chaucer. Anyway, Jun reported that the broadcast itself was very confusing as it never mentioned the word surrender, but he seems to think that the Emperor was ending the war."

"Is that so?" Smitty said. "Well, until we can be completely sure about this, we should sit tight and not disclose any of this information to anyone outside of our immediate group."

Could it be true? Was the war really over?

Smitty didn't have to wait long to verify the content of Emperor Hirohito's broadcast. Early the next morning

Sparks and Jun Lei picked up the same transmission again except this time it broadcast in English by Tadaichi Hirakawa.

Smitty and a few others were immediately awakened and brought in to hear the transmission for ourselves.

TO OUR GOOD AND LOYAL SUBJECTS: After pondering deeply the general trends of the world and the actual conditions obtaining in our empire today, we have decided to effect a settlement of the present situation by resorting to an extraordinary measure. We have ordered our government to communicate to the governments of the United States, Great Britain, China and the Soviet Union that our empire accepts the provisions of their Joint Declaration. To strive for the common prosperity and happiness of all nations as well as the security and well-being of our subjects is the solemn obligation which has been handed down by our imperial ancestors and which lies close to our heart. Indeed, we declared war on America and Britain out of our sincere desire to ensure Japan's self-preservation and the stabilization of East Asia, it being far from our thought either to infringe upon the sovereignty of other nations or to embark upon territorial aggrandizement. But now the war has lasted for nearly four years. Despite the best that has been done by everyone— the gallant fighting of the military and naval forces, the diligence and assiduity of our servants of the state, and the devoted service of our one hundred million people—the war situation has developed not necessarily to Japan's advantage, while the general trends of the world have all turned against her interest. Moreover, the enemy has begun to employ a new and most cruel bomb, the power of which to do damage is, indeed, incalculable, taking the toll of many innocent lives. Should we continue to fight, not only would it result in an ultimate collapse and obliteration of the Japanese nation, but also it would lead to the total extinction of human civilization. Such being the case, how are we to save the millions of our subjects, or to atone ourselves before the hallowed spirits of our imperial ancestors? This is the reason why we have ordered the acceptance of the provisions of the Joint Declaration of the Powers. We cannot but express the deepest sense of regret to our allied nations of East Asia, who have consistently cooperated with the empire toward the emancipation of East Asia. The thought of those officers and men as well as others who have fallen in the fields of battle, those who died at their posts of duty, or those who met with untimely death and all their bereaved families, pains our heart night and day. The welfare of the wounded and the war-sufferers, and of those who have lost their homes and livelihood, are the objects of our profound solicitude. The hardships and sufferings to which our nation is to be subjected hereafter will be certainly great. We are keenly aware of the inmost feelings of all of you, our subjects. However, it is according to the dictates of time and fate that we have resolved to pave the way for a grand peace for all the generations to come by enduring the unendurable and suffering what is insufferable. Having been able to safeguard and maintain the structure of the imperial state, we are always with you, our good and loyal subjects, relying upon your sincerity and integrity. Beware most strictly of any outbursts of emotion which may engender needless complications, or any fraternal contention and strike which may create confusion, lead you astray and cause you to lose the confidence of the world. Let the entire nation continue as one family from generation to generation, ever firm in its faith in the imperishability of its sacred land, and mindful of its heavy burden of responsibility, and of the long road before it. Unite your total strength, to be devoted to construction for the future. Cultivate the ways of rectitude, foster nobility of spirit, and work with resolution – so that you may enhance the innate glory of the imperial state and keep

pace with the progress of the

world."

When the broadcast ended, everyone remained silent and looked to Smitty for clarification. He looked around the barracks at the lot of us then raised his arms to the heavens and with tears of joy streaming down his face. "Praise Jesus, the war is really over."

The room erupted in joyful happiness.

Sparks and Smitty hugged each other and jumped up and down, Smitty's spindly legs looking as if they could snap in two at any moment. After a brief yet heartfelt celebration, Smitty shushed us, urging us to calm ourselves.

"Now look, fellas, not a word of this to anyone right now except Father Charlie and the other Commanders, okay? We have no idea what the Japs know or how they're going to react. We've just got to let it play itself out on their terms. They're the ones still holding the guns to our heads, war or no war."

Smitty's order to calm down and compose ourselves was emotionally difficult and hard to comply with, but it was nonetheless sage advice.

We knew the Japs had heard about Hiroshima and Nagasaki. We also believed that they knew that the war had ended. This might or might not play into our favor. The best outcome we could hope for was that the Japs, realizing that they had lost the war, might try to improve their chances of post war survival by immediately treating us better and improving our desperate conditions.

The worst outcome would be that the Japs, in some sort of utter fanatical despair, killed us all. Every prisoner in any POW camp, whether located in either in the European or Pacific theaters, feared the dreaded *Kill All Order*. It was a well-known fact that the Nazis executed prisoners all of the time and that recently the Japs had done the same to one hundred fifty allied prisoners on Palawan Island in the Philippines. It didn't take an enormous stretch of the imagination to think of the dastardly and sadistic plans Mesuga and Bonecracker might have in store for us at the very end. Rumor regarding what could happen to us in our final days was rampant and disturbing.

The next morning, Mesuga took to the camp public address system while everyone stood outside at attention. "I know that things here have been hard for everyone. A new camp has just been completed near here and already some of your comrades have been taken there. Soon, the rest of you will join them. Ample food and medical care is yours for the asking at the new camp. No prisoner will have labor forced on them there. This great gift bestowed on you by the Imperial Nation of Japan is given because of the Emperor's great empathy for your plight. Because I share that same empathy with our supreme leader, I have arranged for an immediate and expeditious transfer of everyone to this much improved camp."

"That's bollocks," Smitty said to us once we were back in our barracks. Scuttlebutt is that villagers have seen bodies in the jungle. Mesuga's lie is designed to lure us into the jungle and to our deaths. Maybe he'll say we were trying to escape. Spread the word, mates. We're not going to make it easy for Mesuga to implement a *Kill All Order*. Those bastards might have the guns, but there are more of us than them. We'll simply refuse to march and they won't dare to kill us all here in the camp. Mesuga knows he can't get away with that."

Word spread quickly and by sundown not one of us had been marched away. For now, we were winning our game of chicken with Mesuga.

The next day, August 15th, was the last time we saw Lieutenant Colonel Mesuga in camp. The Japs continued to burn records and were now destroying much of their equipment as well. A huge bonfire raged in the middle of their compound and it looked like they'd torched just about everything.

Around noon Smitty and I saw Mesuga rushing out of his office holding a suitcase and a handful of papers clutched against his chest. He was driven off in that same big black Chrysler he'd previously used to return the mangled Bunny to camp. As the dust settled from Mesuga's quick departure, a horrible realization swept over me.

Now that Mesuga was gone, the Bonecracker was in charge, at least until he, too, fled the camp with his tail between his legs. Mesuga might not have the balls to kill us all within the confines of camp but Tagata certainly did.

Strangely, the war's end hadn't seemed to faze Tagata all that much except that now, four Jap guards accompanied him wherever he went. Before this day, he'd strutted about Batu Lintang unprotected as if he was the biggest, baddest rooster in all of Borneo, as if he feared nothing and no one. But now that Mesuga was gone, he seemed more cautious and calculating in his movements as the presence of constant bodyguards seemed to attest.

It snowed in Borneo on August 16th. The flakes were huge rectangles covered in black ink. JAPAN HAS SURRENDERED each flake proclaimed. The snow fluttered from the sky courtesy of three Bristol DAP Beaufighter airplanes. It was the most beautiful snowfall I'd ever seen.

Now everyone knew that the war was over—really and truly over—every prisoner, every civilian, every Jap. The entire camp went berserk—hundreds of worn-out, bedraggled, skeletons, hugging each other, crying out their happiness.

Outraged at the prisoners' joyous reactions, Tagata ordered his men to fire a few rounds just over the heads of the dancing prisoners. We fell to the ground, covering our heads with our arms. "War not over, war not over!" Tagata shouted over the camp's loud speakers.

"This propaganda. Return to barracks immediately!"

When Tagata's rant was finished, all the captives rushed inside their own barrack. Until then, I'd never seen a time when at least some people weren't milling about the compound. Now, not a single prisoner remained outside, each shuttered inside, most likely waiting for what was going to happen next.

The camp was largely quiet for the rest of the evening yet inside my barrack we exchanged excited whispers between each other. After a while, I noticed a sound different from the shared whispers. A scratchy sound like the distinctive popping noise of a needle being placed on a record emanated from the speakers strung throughout the camp.

"What was that?" I said to no one and everyone near me.

Before anyone could say a word, a beautiful, deep operatic voice began singing in Italian.

Nessun dorma! Nessun dorma! Tu pure, o, Principessa, nella tua fredda stanza, guardi le stele, che tremano d'amore, e di speranza. Ma il mio mistero è chiuso in me, il nome mio nessun saprà! No, no, sulla tua bocca lo dirò quando la luce splenderà! Ed il mio bacio scioglierà il silenzio che ti fa mia! (Il nome suo nessun saprà!e noi dovrem, ahime, morir!)Dilegua, o notte! Tramontate, stele! Tramontate, stele! All'alba vincerò! vincerò, vincerò!

My heart raced and I began to tremble. "No, no, no," I repeated over and over as I hauled myself off of my sleeping mat.

"Pipe down, Flyer," Smitty said. "What's wrong?"

I shook my head. "Those Jap bastards wouldn't do such a thing, not now. The war is fucking over."

Smitty had come along my side and now he grabbed me. "What in the hell is the matter with you?

"That song is the problem. It's *Nessun Dorma!*"

310

His face remained blank. "What's the deal with Nessun whatever?"

"Here's a rough translation of the lyrics, mate, and I warn you now, you're not going to like them."

> "*Nobody shall sleep! Nobody shall sleep! Even you, o Princess, in your cold room, watch the stars that tremble with love and with hope. But my secret is hidden within me, my name no one shall know. No! No! On your mouth I will tell it when the light shines. And my kiss will dissolve the silence that makes you mine! (No one will know his name and we must, alas, die.) Vanish, o night!*

Set, stars! Set, stars! At

dawn, I will win! I will win! I

will win!"

"What are you going on about, Flyer. It's just some old opera song. I know the singing isn't too good, but it's not so bad that you have to get your knickers in such a wad."

"It's not the singing that bothers me, it's the words. You see this particular opera is about a cold-hearted princess named Turandot. Any man who wants to marry her must first answer three extremely difficult questions. No one ever has ever successfully answered these questions until this one man called the Calaf does. However, seeing that the princess still doesn't want to marry him, he then offers his own proposal. If Turandot can successfully guess the mysterious Calaf's name by sunrise the next morning she can execute him and be done with the matter once and for all. The evil princess orders all of her subjects to help discover his name by morning, threatening them all with death if they don't succeed. Nobody shall sleep tonight she orders. Don't you see, Smitty? Turandot had issued a kill all order, and whoever the sick bastard is who's playing this record at the other end of this transmission is trying to send us a not so subtle message."

"You don't really think—"

"That we're all going to be killed? Maybe, I don't know."

Smitty stared at the ground. Breaking the somber mood he asked "Well, did she ever discover his name?"

"What?"

"The Calaf, did she ever find out his name?"

"Yes, she did." I laughed a bit.

"Well, what was it?" he asked.

I smiled. "Love. His name was Love."

"That's why I fucking hate the opera." Shaking his head from side to side, Smitty turned and walked away.

I lay down and thought about Bunny. I stared at the ceiling but imagined the stars that I knew were directly above me even if I couldn't see them. I had a friend in the stars and he would keep a watch over me. As I felt my eyes becoming heavy, I began to chant to myself, 'vincero, vincero, vincero.'

Someone, Tagata probably, played Nessun Dorma over and over again all night long. I woke up tired and tormented, but was never so happy to see a sunrise. I'd made it through another night at Batu Lantang. There was still hope.

After most of the prisoners in my longhouse had awakened, we decided to venture cautiously outside, into the central compound. It was strangely quiet. There was little sound except for the shuffling of feet, the occasional cough, or a hushed whisper. I guess a few hundred of us were milling about, trying to figure out what was going on, when the main gate into the prisoners' compound slowly creaked opened.

A conscripted Korean guard drove a large, mule drawn cart into the center of the camp. On the flatbed, a canvas covered an equally large lump of something.

"Tagata gone, war over, really over," the guard named Gi Mee Soon, whom we simply called Jimmy, said in broken English. He pulled back the canvas and smiled at us. A pile of food, medicine, and water comprised the mound.

I felt my legs go weak. This was so unbelievable. There were eggs and meat, some bread and fruits of all kind. The Korean guards had emptied the food pantry for us!

I looked toward the heavens and smiled.

"Thanks, Bunny. *Vincero!*"

"Please take," Jimmy said. "Enjoy." He sprinted out the front gate, not bothering to shut it behind himself.

By this time, hundreds of prisoners jammed the center of the compound. They surged toward the food without warning, a starving horde of survivors who'd suddenly lost their minds. A man from my longhouse was knocked to the ground and trampled by his brethren. His screams, along with those of the mob, might have rivaled those of all the people ever trapped in hell. Everyone wanted some of the food that was barely abundant enough to feed a hundred people.

Smitty had just climbed onto the cart when, coming from every possible direction, the stampede of prisoners began.

"No, no, no! Smitty," I yelled, hands cupped against my lips. "Jump off!"

The first of the rioters, their frenzied fingers grasping and clawing at whatever they could, overran the cart a few seconds later.

The blow to Smitty's legs came out of nowhere or perhaps came from everywhere. It was hard to tell with so many arms swinging toward the mound of food. There one second and then gone the next, Smitty disappeared within the mass of prisoners pressed against the cart.

I fought my way toward him. It was like trying to penetrate a brick wall with only my fists. Curiously though, the closer I got to where I thought the cart was located, the easier going it became, and it wasn't until I reached my goal that I discovered why.

Every last morsel of food and water and all the medical supplies were gone, and those lucky few prisoners who'd managed to snatch any of the booty were quickly moving away from the cart with smaller frenzied mobs in pursuit.

As one man tried to shove what looked like an entire loaf of bread in his mouth lest he have to share any of it, two other men tried to wrench it away from him.

Hunks of bread hit the ground and were trampled in the melee.

Fistfights had begun to break out all around me. Few people seemed to have gotten much, if anything from the cart, and now the disgruntled were taking out their frustrations on their comrades.

The sight sickened me but not enough to cause me to intervene in any of the fights. My one and only goal now was to find Smitty.

People continued to come toward the cart but not like before. And when they saw that nothing was left they moved away. I climbed on the cart, hoping to get a better view of the grounds overtop of the heads of everyone. I desperately hoped that I'd see Smitty off in the distance, safe and sound.

When I jumped down, my foot got caught on one of the spokes of the wheel. I felt myself falling before I could get my hands all the way out in front of me. I landed on my side, next to one of the cart wheels.

Without even lifting my head off of the ground, I saw Smitty's body lying under the center of the vehicle. He wasn't moving.

"Oh, God. Smitty." I tugged at his arm, eventually wresting him from his hidden place. As he slowly regained consciousness, I asked "You okay?"

"What happened, mate?" Smitty asked as I helped him stand up. A large bump was noticeable on his forehead. "Feels like a ton of bricks hit me."

"A stampede is what happened," I said. "Everyone went mad, fighting over food, forgetting that we're all in the same boat. And after all you've done for them, you and Sparks and his men, well, I just can't believe that they tried to kill you."

"Don't worry about me, Flyer. It wasn't personal. I know that. You know that. These people are starving. So are you. So am I."

"Yeah, but—"

Smitty interrupted me.

"Let it go son, just let it all go."

Chapter Thirty-One

A day after the food riot, Smitty and the other barracks' commanders took stock of the camp's remaining food. The news wasn't good. Supplies were running dangerously low. Though the camp leaders put in place a draconian food rationing policy, Smitty figured that we would be completely out of food in less than a week. Even with the noble assistance of the local villagers, feeding hundreds of starving prisoners was no easy task.

Batu Lintang quickly became an open camp. Pro-allied villagers, primarily ethnic Chinese, brought enormous amounts of rice and fruit into the camp to help sustain us over the next few days. Smitty continued to organize and restore order. Food and medicine were first distributed to those who needed it most. Most all of the former prisoners abided by this policy, and the ones who didn't were dealt with by Smitty's *Golden God's*, proving that sometimes, might does make right.

We now used the Old Lady, aka Mrs. Harris, around the clock as information about the end of the war continued to pour in. Two bits of information that were of particular interest to the prisoners of Batu Lintang dominated the airwaves.

First, we learned that General Douglas MacArthur, the Supreme Allied Commander in the Pacific, had issued General Order Number One, which required the Japanese to provide information regarding the exact locations of all Allied prisoner of war camps. The Japs were also told that they were directly responsible for the well-being and safety of Allied prisoners and were instructed to provide all necessary food, shelter, and medicines needed to carry out this order.

Secondly, we were informed that the Allied invasion of Borneo had actually begun on May 1, 1945—thirty days before *Betty Grable's Ass* had crashed—and that Allied troops had landed just to the north of us in Brunei around the tenth of June. The Australian 9th Division was currently advancing toward Kuching, less than twenty five miles from us.

By August 30th, many of the anxious prisoners, including myself, were becoming increasingly angry and disheartened as each day passed with no rescue. Where was the 9th Division? Why had they forsaken us?

Just when we were at our lowest point and about to abandon all hope, a Douglas Dakota seaplane appeared and began circling high above Batu Lintang. We all cheered wildly as the first of twenty white parachutes popped out of the plane and began its slow descent toward the ground.

"There's another one," prisoners yelled and pointed as each chute opened up. It was like watching puppies being born, strange looking things popping out all over the place! We called the bounty from the sky 'storepedoes.' These metal canisters, long and shaped like a torpedo, were filled with just about every provision you could think of— bread, canned meat, cigarettes, chocolate, and other sweets. It was quite literally manna from heaven. We had been saved once again and this time without an impromptu riot.

Each canister usually had a handwritten message emblazoned on its side—saying things like *'we know where you are;' 'on our way to get you;'* and *'hold on.'* The messages alone were enough to buoy our spirits. Imagine our delight when even more storpedoes arrived a few days later. It was now early September and it looked like we might really make it after all.

As we waited for our now imminent rescue, Bunny's death continued to haunt me every day and kept me awake long hours of the night. Come hell or high water,

I would avenge his death starting with the two people I held personally responsible—Mesuga and the Bonecracker.

Since the Japs fled, I had painstakingly wandered around the Batu Lintang, collecting every single piece of evidence that I thought might be used against Mesuga, Tagata, and their henchmen if they were ever found and brought before a war crimes tribunal. Although I did a general search over the entire camp, I concentrated my efforts in the area formerly occupied by Mesuga and Tagata and the other Japanese officers.

Pretty much everything had been smashed to pieces or burned or sometimes both. One afternoon, while inspecting what looked to be a part of a severely damaged metal desk, I pulled open one of its bent up drawers and saw it.

Bonecracker's ball-peen hammer.

At first I just stared at it, remembering the horrific damage it was used for. Eventually, I stuffed it into my sack.

I shuffled through the remains of the other metal drawers with little success. I was about to call it a day and go have a long rest under Bunny's tree when I spied a broken picture frame lying face down on the ground. When I picked it up, what remained of its broken glass in the front fell out, revealing a slightly scorched black and white photo.

My heart began to race as I studied the image closer.

Mesuga.

He was posed in a Samurai warrior uniform, his hand clutching a sword. He looked much younger and thinner than I remembered him as Commander of Batu Lintang. The photo, most likely, had been taken at the beginning of the war, perhaps as early as the Japanese invasion of Manchuria in 1937.

Now, I had a photograph of Mesuga, and that's all the evidence I needed.

Littered amongst the decimated wreck of what had to have been his office, I also found a tattered rising sun desk flag and an unopened pack of Japanese cigarettes. I crammed everything into my pack.

September 11, 1945 was the day of our liberation. Around 2:30 in the afternoon, Sparks informed Smitty that he'd learned via Mrs. Harris that Major General Hiyoe Yamamura had surrendered all Japanese military forces in Kuching and that Australian forces were now in control of the entire area.

Smitty looked at me and smiled. "It won't be long now, mate."

I'd heard that line before, again and again, over the past two weeks.

Two hours later, an incredible rumbling noise could be heard along the jungle road. It felt almost like a small earthquake, as powerful vibrations began to move from my feet up through my legs.

The Australian 9th Division had arrived.

"It's time to go home, fellas!" Smitty cried out.

The central compound instantly filled with cheering men and women from all of the barracks, as everyone ran to greet our liberators.

The Australians entered Batu Lintang looking like conquering Roman gladiators. Flags flew and bagpipers piped, and the entire lot was accompanied by four huge armored transport vehicles laden with food and medicine just for us. Major General George Wootten, Commander of the Australian 9th Division, rode at the front of the relief column. Never had I seen such a more distinguished looking fellow.

The cacophony emanating from the former prisoners became so loud I thought my ears might start to bleed. To say that we were ecstatic was an understatement. We had survived Batu Lintang, Mesuga and the Bonecracker, and now we could all head home. It was an absolutely euphoric madhouse.

The Australians first order of business was to set up a field hospital to take care of the most severely sick and malnourished prisoners in the camp. They set about building showers and digging latrines. Each prisoner was given a cot with a mattress. The feeling of sleeping on something soft once again was so unfamiliar that I actually slept on my floor mat for the first three nights.

Over the next few days, most of the healthy prisoners like me helped with the feeding and comforting of the most severely afflicted among us. I felt like Walt Whitman during the Civil War, as I gave my fellow comrades-in-arms sponge baths and shaved their faces.

Although I stayed extremely busy, I couldn't shake or even stem the hatred I felt for Mesuga and Tagata. Knowing that they were still free irked me to no end. My need for a day of reckoning, a time when unsettled scores demanded their retribution, grew into an obsession as foul as a festering, pus-filled sore. For the truly wronged such as I was, real satisfaction could only be found in one of two places: absolute forgiveness or mortal vindication.

I did not have it within me to grant the first.

I set about planning how I would achieve the second.

Chapter Thirty-Two

Ironically, a large portion of Batu Lintang was now being used to detain the ever increasing numbers of captured Japanese soldiers being brought in daily. Former allied prisoners were being freed and Japanese prisoners were being detained. Smitty and the other camp leaders were adamant that they would not stand for any violent reprisals against the Japs or the Korean conscripts now under Australian supervision. For the most part, everyone abided by the new camp rules because they knew that many of the guards had operated under the duress of Japanese conscription and, for the most part, had not committed any serious crimes against any allied prisoner. Smitty assured everyone, that military war crimes tribunals would deal with everything now and that under no circumstances were we to take matters of retribution into our own hands.

Nevertheless, I couldn't keep myself away from the fenced off area where the Jap prisoners were kept. All day, I searched the faces of the incoming prisoners, on the lookout for Mesuga and Tagata. The number of prisoners steadily grew. Eventually, the Jap prisoner population surpassed what ours had been when we were the ones behind the barbed wire.

One afternoon, as I stared through the fence, an Australian guard walked up to me and handed me a lit cigarette. "You look like you could use this more than me, mate."

"Thanks." I took the cigarette and inhaled deeply. Ah, an unfiltered Camel. Just like Bunny smoked. "Dammit," I said, tears suddenly welling in my eyes. I turned my head and brushed them away.

"You okay?" the guard asked.

"I'm fine."

"It's just that I've seen you looking in here for the past three days. Something on your mind, Yank?"

"I'm looking for a Korean guard who was especially kind to me and my buddies," I lied. "I want to put in a good word for him. But I haven't yet been able to find him."

"He might be in the other POW camp," the Aussie said.

"Oh? Where is that?"

"Just outside of Kuching, about twenty miles from here. Maybe the Korean's there."

For the first time in days I felt myself grin, and it felt damned good. "I guess I won't know until I look."

I took another drag on the cigarette then handed it back to the guard. "Thanks."

I approached Smitty, unsure what I was going to say. I knew I couldn't come right out and admit that I was going to go hunt down and execute the Jap bastards who'd murdered Bunny. He'd made it clear that the war crime tribunals would handle all matters of revenge and that any reprisals by allied troops would be met with incarceration.

But I had to go and the sooner the better.

I found Smitty sitting with a few of his closest advisors. I motioned to him. "Hey, can I talk to you for a sec?"

Smitty excused himself and walked toward me. "What's on your mind, mate?"

"I think it's time for me to go. There's nothing left for me here, no other Americans, I mean. I need to get back with my own lot so I can head home, back to the states."

"You're right about that. You have no superior officer here to whom you must report. But you're wrong when you say you have nothing left here. We've got each other, you, me, the other fellas, Father Charlie. Hell, we can become one great big jungle family. This place can be our new, happy home." He chuckled and slapped me on the back.

"Well, you know I appreciate that, Smitty. I'd absolutely love to stay, I mean you know how much I love it here," I said with ultra-fake sincerity.

"Sure, you do, mate." Smitty winked at me.

"All kidding aside I knew it was about time for you to head out."

"I guess so," I said.

"You know, if my best friend had been murdered like yours was, I'd want to find the sons of bitches responsible. Word of advice, though. Don't get caught. It would be a shame to let the Japs have the last laugh. You understand what I mean, Alex?"

He never called me Alex.

My arms were around him in an instant and I hugged him tight. After a moment, I stepped back and shook his hand.

"Thanks, Colonel. I'll never forget you and what you did for the men of Batu Latang." I snapped off a salute, which he crisply returned.

Smitty helped me find some new clothes and even bartered with one of the Australians guards for one of his captured Japanese pistols. I don't know what he traded for it, but I sure was grateful. The next day I packed all of my belongings into a knapsack and exited the longhouse. I made sure to include all of the evidence I had collected throughout the camp. Before I exited our barrack for the final time, Smitty called his men to attention.

My eyes immediately filled with tears. Some of the men were so infirm that they were barely able to stand at attention, and yet here they were giving me a real military send off. I had served my time in hell with some of the finest people to ever walk the earth, and I was going to miss them terribly.

I shook each man's hand and saluted him. When I finally got to Smitty, I didn't know what to say. He'd saved my life while incarcerated in Batu Lintang. He extended his hand to me. "Well, Yank, I guess this is goodbye for now."

"I guess so," I said. "I don't really know how to thank you for everything you've done."

"No worries, mate. Here." He handed me a piece of paper. "I've written down all my information for you. I hope that one day we can meet again." He looked me directly in the eyes. "The war's over, what was done was done. Do what you need to do and then try to let it all go and get on with your life. Try to find a way to see the world as something other than menacing blackness, Flyer, like you saw it before the war. Will you do that for me, for Bunny?"

"Okay, I'll give it my best shot." We hugged again and then I turned and walked through the gates of Batu Lintang. I turned around and looked at the camp one last time then closed my eyes tight, storing a mental snapshot within my brain.

Smitty had dispensed sage advice that I'm sure would serve me well in life, but I also knew that there was no one right way to peace, I would have to find my own path according to my own life experience, just like the Buddha had done. I would never be able to get on with my life until I fulfilled my promise to avenge Bunny. And, for better or worse, that was exactly what I was about to do.

Chapter Thirty-Three

In addition to the Jap pistol, my knapsack also contained a Japanese bayonet, one slightly ripped, flowered-print shirt that I found on the ground back at Batu Lintang, obviously left behind by one of the fleeing Jap guards, a tiny amount of gold that Smitty had given to me in case of an emergency, and a signed paper documenting who I was, what had happened to me, and where I was going. I also carried all the items I'd scavenged from the Mesuga and Tegata's offices.

I traveled by foot as I made my way toward the city of Kuching and the enormous Japanese POW camp that had been hastily thrown up on the city's outskirts. All along the way I passed hundreds of Jap prisoners on the side of the road. They were, for the most part, only lightly guarded by Australian troops. Beaten and battered, they didn't seem much of a threat now. In fact, it seemed that most of them were happy the war was over and that they would soon be heading home. I well understood that feeling and yet I wasn't anxious to immediately head back to the states. Not until I had my revenge.

If I didn't find Mesuga or Tagata at this camp, I would search another and another, and I wouldn't stop searching until I found them. They were either going to face justice via a military tribunal or by me. I just hadn't figured out which one yet. In the meantime, I decided that if neither Mesuga nor Tagata were in Kuching, I'd return to Bunny's Z-force jungle encampment and retrieve his wedding ring, the photo of him and his wife on the beach, and my high school class ring.

Along the way to Kuching I inspected every Japanese prisoner I ran across though always without success. After two days, without any luck, I arrived at the makeshift POW camp. In fact, I smelled it before I actually saw it. The horrendous odor of the accumulated human waste of thousands of Jap prisoners nauseated me. The air also reeked with the smoke and stench of wood fires that were lit to burn just about everything. How anyone could stand it, I did not know.

Nevertheless, I approached the camp gate with jaunty steps.

"Stop right there," one of the Aussie soldiers called out when I was within ten feet of the guardhouse. "State your business."

"Technical Sergeant Alex Anderson of the 408th Squadron out of Brisbane."

"You're not from Oz, mate. You sound like a damn Yank."

"That's because I am a damn Yank. You can call me Flyer."

"So what do you want, Flyer? This is an enemy combatant camp. You need to go to the field headquarters in order to arrange for your transportation back home. No one here can help you."

"Actually, I'm trying to find someone."

The guard looked at me like I had a screw loose.

I held my hands out to him, in supplication. "I just need to get inside the camp and have a look around. You see, I'm looking for two particular Japs. We have a some unfinished business to take care of."

"Uh, huh. What kind of unfinished business?"

I figured honesty was the best policy.

"Well, you see, those little Nip cocksuckers murdered my best friend while we were in a POW camp about twenty or so miles from here. I want to find him and make sure that he's one of the first ones to be brought up on war crime charges. I owe it to my buddy."

I must have said the magic words, because the gate opened up for me a minute later.

Even though I was alone among hundreds of Jap prisoners I didn't feel threatened at all. I carried my pistol in my right hand and the damaged photo of Mesuga in the other, as I walked brazenly throughout the camp. Every so often I held up the photo and asked the Jap POWs if they had seen him.

No one had.

After a few hours of searching, dusk began to descend in smoky veils that drained most of the color from the world. I decided not to press my luck in the dark with the Japs. After all, there were a whole lot more of them than there were of me. I headed back toward the front gate.

As I approached the front gate to exit, I saw a familiar face out of the corner of my eye.

The Bonecracker stood less than five feet from me.

I raised my pistol and aimed it at his face.

He looked directly at me, and then that old sadistic smile appeared. "You can't do anything, Yankee. I go home. War over." He smirked.

It would have been so easy and ever so satisfying to blow his fucking brains out.

As my index finger tightened on the trigger, the Australian guard who'd let me in, suddenly appeared right next to me.

"Easy, boy-o." He reached for my arm and slowly pushed it toward the ground. "What are you doing, mate? You'll get thrown in the brig for that. You've been in prison long enough. It's not worth it. Identify him to the tribunal, give them all your evidence, and be done with it."

Tagata and some of the other nips nearby were now laughing at me.

"Still a Yankee coward," Tagata yelled out as the guard escorted me through the front gate.

The Aussie released my arm and stared at me. "Don't come back for your own sake, mate. Just stay the hell away. He'll get what's coming to him."

I pulled myself together and grudgingly walked away, across the unpaved road to the make-shift bar filled with Australians in varying degrees of inebriation.

I ordered a warm beer and waited for the guards to end their shift. I had a proposition for them that I hoped they would take.

A couple of hours later, I saw a changing of the guards at the gate and in the surrounding watch towers. The guard with whom I'd had the earlier encounters and another one crossed the road, headed toward the bar.

I watched them order their beers and then sit at a small table recently vacated by another group of men.

I approached them cautiously.

"Hey, fellas, remember me?"

They looked up at me. "C'mon buddy," the one who'd thrown me out of the camp said. "Not you again."

"If I could just have a second." I hated my own whining, begging tone. But I knew that I needed to connect with him, man to man, soldier to soldier.

He waved me down to a chair at their table. "What?"

"That Jap back there in the camp—"

"You mean the one who pretty much called you a pussy right to your face?" The guard sighed and sipped his beer.

"Uh, yeah that's the one all right. His name is Tagata. Back at the POW camp we just called him the Bonecracker."

"What camp are you talking about?"

"Batu Lintang," I said.

"You were in Batu Lintang?" he asked.

"Indeed I was, and that fucking monster back there killed, maimed and tortured many prisoners, most of whom were Australian just like you."

I could see that what I was now telling them was having an impact. I wished I had the picture of Bunny and his wife to show them, but I didn't since I hadn't gone back to the jungle camp yet to retrieve it.

"They murdered my best friend. His name was Bunny Hobson and he was an Aussie from Manly Beach."

"I've been to Manly Beach before," one of the men said. "It's nice."

"Yeah, that's what Bunny said. Anyway, Bunny was a member of Z-force." I looked down at my hands as I felt myself getting emotional. "He was one of the best," I whispered.

"He did some damn good work over here too. He killed a lot of Japs and saved my life and the lives of many other people."

One of the guards took a deep breath. "Look, buddy, I'm sorry for what happened to your mate, but what can we do?"

I pulled out the little bit of gold Smitty had given me and pushed it across the table, in front of them.

"This in exchange for him." I searched the faces of the men.

They looked at each other and then glanced around the bar, probably checking to see if anyone might be watching us. I knew I was putting them in a terribly awkward, if not downright dangerous, position.

"I don't know," one of the guards said. "That's a pretty big request. We could get into a shitload of trouble."

"I know and believe me, I'm terribly sorry to have to ask, but I made a promise. That son of a bitch maimed dozens of Allied prisoners by smashing them with a ball-peen hammer."

I reached into my knapsack and pulled it out to show them.

"This hammer."

Both of the Australians grimaced as they stared at the instrument of destruction.

"He strangled my best friend to death right in front of me and a hundred other prisoners. That son of a bitch deserves what he's got coming. You're my only hope, please fellas."

I guess they could see in my eyes how desperate I was, because the next thing they said really surprised me.

"Okay."

"Yeah, okay," the other guard said.

At first I thought I had misunderstood them, but I hadn't.

"Tomorrow night, right after dark, just before we get off, we'll blindfold and tie up the dirty pig and tell him that he's being taken up to headquarters for interrogation.

It's common protocol to bind and blindfold prisoners when we take them outside of the camp. Nobody should suspect anything. You wait for us where the jungle road meets the old beach road and we'll turn him over to you then, okay?"

"Perfect," I said.

"I don't know how to thank you guys."

"No worries, mate," one of them said, sounding just like Bunny. We finished our beers and shook hands.

As we got up to leave I saw the gold still on the table.

"Don't forget that." I pointed to the gold.

They looked at each other, smiled, and one of them reached over and pushed it back toward me. "No charge, mate, this one's on us."

Around eight the next night, I saw in the distance the two Australian guards escorting the blindfolded Bonecracker toward me on the jungle road where I waited. My heart raced with anticipation. I was finally going to confront the sadistic Jap prison guard about his torturous past.

Not a word was spoken as the exchange was made. Neither the Australians nor I smiled. We just nodded and went our separate ways.

Captain Hideo Tagata—the Bonecracker—was now in my hands and he didn't even know it.

We walked for about an hour.

Tagata must have become suspicious about what was happening because his pace slowed.

I pulled the ball-peen hammer from my backpack, then grabbed Tagata's bound hands and let him feel the long wooden handle and the heavy steel-tipped hammer at the top of the shaft.

A thrill surged through me when I was sure that he recognized it.

He fell to the ground. "No, no, no," he shouted.

As soon as he opened his mouth to take another breath before screaming again, I gagged him with an oil-soaked rag I'd found on the road to Kuching. He thrashed his head from side to side.

I attempted to get him back onto his feet, but he refused.

I raised the ball-peen hammer without thinking and brought it down with as much force as I could onto his left elbow. The Bonecracker let loose a blood-curdling scream then slumped face-first onto the ground. I'd shattered his elbow into a thousand broken pieces. It felt good.

Eventually I got him back up onto his feet and moving forward again. I estimate we tramped along that deserted beach road for at least seven more hours. The great Samurai warrior, whimpered and sniffled like a little child for most of the way. He must have mumbled the word 'please' in both English and Japanese a dozen times.

I briefly considered smashing the hammer against his teeth to shut him the fuck up.

Finally, just before sunrise, we reached a spot where the jungle ended and the beach began. It was the perfect clearing. The full moon was quickly sinking in the night sky and the morning trade winds had already started to make the palm leaves dance back and forth above our heads.

I bent over toward Tagata. "We're here," I whispered to him in Japanese. With sunrise just about to occur, I set about organizing the tiny jungle stage for what might be my final performance in Borneo.

For just a brief moment I was overcome with an incredible feeling of doubt and had terrible reservations about what I was intending to do. It was the same exact feeling that I had when I pointed my pistol at him at the POW camp. I couldn't pull the trigger then, could I pull it now?

My lifelong adherence to the teachings of Jesus Christ and his admonition to love and forgive my enemies plagued my every thought. Question after question streamed through my mind. Would carrying out this assassination—because that's exactly what it was, plain and simple murder—would this haunt me forever and brand me as yet another Christian hypocrite?

Using the fog of war excuse for my actions would assuage some of my guilt, but certainly not all of it. For God's sake if Shakespeare suggested that we become like God when 'mercy seasons justice,' what in the hell was I about to do?

I could just walk away and leave the Bonecracker in this clearing, next to the beach. I could try to pretend that none of this had ever happened. I could return him to the proper war crime tribunal and let them dispense justice. I had all the evidence needed. But would that be enough?

Oh, Father, what am I to do?

Was revenge for Bunny's death worth eternal damnation of my soul or could I somehow see fit to extend mercy to this most wretched of men?

As I sat on the beach and pondered the fate of my soul, I emptied out the contents of my backpack onto a couple of large palm leaves. While rubbing the ball-peen hammer, I tried to conjure up the image of Bunny from the picture, handsome and healthy, stretched out on the beach with his beautiful wife.

But I couldn't seem to bring that image clearly into focus. Instead, all that my mind's eye would let me see was the beaten and bloodied Bunny after his knee had been smashed, after part of his tongue had been cut out, after his head had been bashed in.

To hell with my soul. Let it be damned. There would be no mercy this day.

I looked at the Bonecracker who was now sitting upright, apparently trying his best to compose himself like the Samurai warrior he proclaimed to be.

Using a small piece of twine, I tied the rising sun desk flag I'd found, around the palm tree in front of the Bonecracker.

I picked up the two wooden handgrips I'd brought with me and meticulously guided the twenty-four inch wire between them. It was just like threading a sewing needle. I tied off the ends once the wire had passed through both grips. My handmade garrote was now ready for use.

I moved closer to the Bonecracker and put my arm around him. He flinched at my touch, but I kept my arm on firmly upon his shoulder. Together we would wait for the sun to come up.

I felt uncontrollable tremors rippling through his body as I watched the waves slowly peel across the distant reef. With each passing second, the horizon became more and more reddish-orange and when I felt the first warm rays of the new dawn touch my face I knew that it was time.

I removed the Bonecracker's blindfold and gag.

When he turned and saw that it was me, his eyes bulged and he began to thrash and flail about, but it was no use. He was safely secured.

Nodding up and down, I smirked while thinking to myself, 'That's right, you sick fuck it's me, your worst nightmare.' I pulled the beast close to me and softly whispered into his ear in crude Japanese. "We lost a lot in this war didn't we? We both came to this island thinking we were one thing and then each of us found out deep down inside that we were actually something else. Strange isn't it?"

I quickly pivoted directly in front of him without ever getting up off of my knees. I wanted to lecture him one last time about his depraved and inhumane behavior at the Batu Lintang POW camp, but, before I began, he looked down at the black cross tattoo on my arm.

"Is Jesus real?" he quietly asked in English.

I briefly went numb all over. His question sent shivers down my spine. I didn't know how to adequately respond.

"Yes, I believe Jesus is real, and because of that, I pray for forgiveness, how about you?"

He didn't answer or perhaps he didn't know how to answer.

We then sat face to face for a few more seconds, staring directly into each other's eyes. At that moment, the Bonecracker seemed to acknowledge his fate or at least I hoped he did.

As the sun was now quickly rising over the horizon I stood up and walked over to the tree and pointed to the 'rising sun' flag of Japan and then back toward the horizon.

The Bonecracker's eyes darted back and forth between the rising sun flag and the rising sun breaking the horizon.

I reached for the garrote then positioned myself behind him.

He now sat ramrod straight, his red, watery eyes focused directly on the horizon. The great Samurai was ready and so was I, the avenging angel of death. Pouncing on Tagata as quickly as a cat would pounce on a mouse, I threw the wire over his head and pulled on the hand-grips as tightly as I could. I drove my right knee into the middle of his back to gain even more leverage.

I could feel muscle and sinew popping throughout his neck and yet all the while he did not struggle. I pulled the wire noose so tight that I feared I might actually sever his head completely from his body.

Eventually, I felt Tagata's body go limp and witnessed the urine in his bladder let loose, staining his pants.

The Bonecracker was dead.

When I released the garrote, Tagata fell face first into the sand. Bright red blood dripped from his neck onto the white sand. I let the murder weapon fall from my hands as I stepped over his crumpled corpse.

Justice or revenge had been served. Which it was, I couldn't rightfully say. Perhaps it was both.

In a rapturous daze, I slowly walked toward the ocean. Along the way I stripped off all of my bloody clothes then waded out into the beautiful blue South China Sea.

The water, although tropical, felt refreshingly cool as I dove under the first wave. When I came up from beneath the surf, I looked out toward the horizon and saw that the sun had completely risen. With one less villain in the world, a new day had begun.

End of Part One

About the Author

Dr. David Pembroke Neff is a Professor of U.S. History with over twenty-two years of teaching experience. He received his undergraduate degree from Jacksonville University in 1984. He holds graduate degrees in History and Liberal Studies from Old Dominion and Georgetown University respectively. He was awarded his Doctorate from George Mason University in 2005. He has been published in The Encyclopedia of Virginia History and the Dictionary of Virginia Biography. He currently resides in Virginia Beach, Virginia with his wife and three children.

Please visit Flyer-The Novel on Facebook for photos, maps and other related items. Also please write a review on the Amazon Kindle E-Books website. It is greatly appreciated.

Flyer: Part Two will be available in late 2015.

*Special thanks to Lauran Strait for all of her essential assistance in bringing *Flyer* to life.

31465487R00202

Made in the USA
Middletown, DE
01 May 2016